Whatever Happened

To Punishment

Edward L. Vockell, PhD
Associate Professor
Education Department
Purdue University Calumet Campus

Accelerated Development Inc.
P. O. Box 667
Muncie, IN 47305

Library of Congress Catalog Card Number: 77-80556

International Standard Book Number: 0-915202-11-5

© Copyright 1977 by Edward L. Vockell

All rights reserved. No part of this book may be reproduced or transmitted in any form or by any means, electronic or mechanical, including photocopying, recording or by any informational storage and retrieval system, without permission in writing from the publisher.

Corporate Editor: Linda K. Davis

Cover: Sally Grim and Bruce Wolowski

Illustrations: Kandy Scheick

Printed in the United States of America
June 1977

For additional copies order from

Accelerated Development Inc.
Publications Division
P. O. Box 667
Muncie, IN 47305

Cost $7.95 plus postage and handling
   in U.S. and Canada add 50 cents
   in other countries, postage depends upon prevailing rates

  Price is subject to change without notice

DEDICATION

This book is dedicated to the memory of my wife, Karen, who died of cancer while the final manuscript was being completed. Without her help and encouragement this book would never have been completed.

PREFACE

Should we punish our children or not? This old question is receiving renewed attention today from parents, teachers, and others entrusted with the care of children. The Supreme Court intensified the controversy with its recent ruling that corporal punishment is not automatically a violation of children's constitutional rights.

All over the country "traditional" schools are springing up. Their avowed purpose is to get back to the "basics" of education and <u>to stress effective discipline</u>. Often this involves relatively severe corporal punishment for misbehavior. These "traditional" schools are filled to the point of overflowing!

At the same time, other groups are campaigning against the harsh punishment of children. These groups maintain that corporal punishment is cruel, and they point out that a child can best develop into a mature, creative adult in a happy, non-repressive environment. Punishment is said to suppress spontaneity.

Both of these viewpoints possess much validity. Upon closer examination, one can see that these positions are not necessarily contradictory. If a type of punishment can be found that can effectively teach children what <u>not</u> to do without suppressing their spontaniety or having other bad results, then the goals of both of the above viewpoints can be reached.

In this book are suggested several types of punishment that can achieve the desired goals. Several approaches to punishment and related strategies of behavior management are examined and attempts are made to present the results of relevant research in a way directly useful to parents and teachers.

The examples in this book often refer to "children" and "students" since it is written most directly for parents and teachers. However, the principles discussed are applicable at all age levels and to very broad social situations. Therefore, the book will be useful not only for parents and teachers, but also for counselors, police officers, judges, coaches, and other social agents interested in changes in human behavior.

Most recent books on behavior management for parents and teachers advocate the use of positive reinforcement. The idea is to reward children for performing desirable behaviors and to eliminate undesirable behaviors by ignoring such activities.

Without being "reactionary," the point of view maintained in the book is that positive reinforcement will work effectively only when used in conjunction with the judicious use of appropriate punishment procedures.

This book has two major purposes

(1) to teach the reader how to use punishment most effectively when punishment is the appropriate technique to use.

(2) to teach the reader how NOT to use punishment--either intentionally or unintentionally--when punishment is not the appropriate technique to use.

Reading this book and implementing its guidelines should not result in harshly restrictive control of children. Rather, by applying the principles in this book, readers should become more aware of what they are doing, punish effectively when punishment is appropriate, and thereby be free to use considerably more positive techniques in the long run.

May 1977   Edward L. Vockell

CONTENTS

DEDICATION iii

PREFACE v

FIGURES ix

TABLES x

1. Why Do We Punish? 1

    Children's Punishment of Other Children 3
    Punishment in the High School 3
    Drastic Punishment 5
    An Explanation of Drastic Punishment 6
    Summary 8

2. The Three Types of Punishment 9

    The Three Types of Punishment 11
    Unintentional Punishment 17
    Shortcomings of Punishment 23
    Principles of Positive Reinforcement 26
    Guidelines for Effective Punishment 33
    Summary 40

3. Negative Reinforcement--Getting Relief 41

    Factors Influencing the Effectiveness of Negative
        Reinforcement 46
    Case Illustrations 47
    Accidental Negative Reinforcement 55
    Occasions for Negative Reinforcement 59
    Summary 60

4. Alternatives to Punishment 61

    Positive Reinforcement of Incompatible Behaviors . . 63
    Extinction 75
    Satiation 85
    Discrimination Training 87
    Differential Reinforcement of Other Behaviors (DRO) . 88
    Differential Reinforcement of Low Rates of
        Responses (DRL) 89
    Stimulus Change 89
    Counterconditioning 91
    Summary 92

5. Special Kinds of Punishment 93

    Systematic Exclusion (Time-Out) 95
    Response Cost 97
    Negative Practice 98
    Overcorrection 100
    Covert Punishment 101
    Vicarious Punishment 103
    Corporal Punishment 105
    Summary 110

6. Avoiding the Punishment Trap 111

    The Punishment Trap 113
    How to Overcome the Punishment Trap 113
    Punishing Ourselves for Punishing 114
    Reinforcing Constructive Alternatives to Punishment . 116
    Analyzing Your Management Strategies 116
    Think Before You Punish 118
    Reinforce Your Improvements 120
    Avoiding Accidental Punishment 122
    Summary 122

7. Summary--When Should I Punish? 125

    The Positive Role of Punishment 127
    How We Punish Ourselves by Refusing to Punish
      Others 128
    When Punishment Should NOT Be Used 130
    Using Inappropriate Techniques by Accident 132
    Comparison of the Various Techniques for Eliminating
      Behaviors 137
    Deciding What To Do 142
    Summary 144

APPENDIX 145

ANNOTATED BIBLIOGRAPHY 165

INDEX 169

ABOUT THE AUTHOR . . . .

****************************ells
                        FIGURES
****

FIGURES

2.1 Three Types of Punishment 13

6.1 Sample Alternative Strategy Graph 121

7.1 Teach A New Behavior 143

****
                            TABLES
****

TABLES

2.1 Some Examples of Positive Reinforcement 27

6.1 A Sample Punishment Chart 117

6.2 Sample Alternative Strategy Chart 121

7.1 Self-punishment through Refusal to Punish 129

7.2 Examples of Accidentally Accomplishing
    Inappropriate Results 133

7.3 Techniques for Reducing or Eliminating Behaviors . . 138

Chapter **1**

WHY DO WE PUNISH ?

****

CONTENTS: Children's Punishment of Other Children

Punishment in the High School

Drastic Punishment

An Explanation of Drastic Punishment

Summary

****

Objective of Chapter 1

The purpose of this introductory Chapter is to present the general framework within which punishment and other control techniques will be discussed in subsequent chapters.

CHILDREN'S PUNISHMENT OF OTHER CHILDREN

Have you ever watched a small group of young children when they decide to "play school"? What do they spend most of their time doing?

Do the older ones help the younger ones?

Sometimes.

Do they sing songs, read books, work math problems, and have recess?

Usually.

But one thing nearly always happens: The "teachers" spend much time <u>punishing</u> the "pupils."

This condition is true even among preschoolers, who have never even seen the inside of a classroom.

The same thing happens when children play "mommies and daddies": the parents spend a huge amount of their time punishing--or rather persecuting--the children.

The reason children exemplify this behavior is because they are thoroughly convinced that deliberate punishment--even very harsh punishment--is one of the distinguishing characteristics of the school or family situation.

PUNISHMENT IN THE HIGH SCHOOL

"I paddled sixteen kids in study hall today. One short of my record."

"If the school board has its way, you're not going to be allowed to do that any more. Some guy in the junior high is being sued because the kid claims he had bruises for two weeks."

"No difference. I don't think paddling is the best way to handle kids anyway. I think the best technique is peer pressure. Make fools of them in front of the whole class."

"Yeah. Yesterday I had a showdown with one of mine during third period. He was looking out the window while I was talking. I stopped my lecture and said, 'If you think you're too smart to pay attention in this class, perhaps you'd like an alternate assignment.' That spoiled brat looked me straight in the eye and mumbled, 'Might as well. I sure as hell ain't learned anything in here so far.' The kid really was trying to put me on the spot. So I walked to the board, drew a circle, and told him, 'OK. I want you to kneel here with your nose inside that circle for the rest of the period.' He did it, too, for forty-five minutes. You can bet he won't try to make a fool of me any more!"

"You gotta break their spirits. Show 'em who's boss."

STOP!!!

This is a biased book!

This book is beginning to sound like the ravings of another "Bleeding Heart Liberal" maintaining that children should never be punished. This book may seem to be saying (like A. S. Neill in Summerhill) that people who punish children do so because they hate children. And you, the reader, are likely to be responding, "That's crazy! Sometimes I punish my children because I love them." or "My parents spanked me when I was a kid, and I'm a better person for it."

Fine! Try not to worry about it. What this book does is focus on some abuses and inadequacies in punishment. By focusing on such topics in the introductory chapter, the intent is to focus more clearly on the important characteristics of punishment. By focusing on these characteristics, you'll be able to

--use punishment more effectively when it is in fact appropriate.

--avoid accidental abuse or misuse of punishment in other situations.

So read on!

DRASTIC PUNISHMENT

Sometimes we even hear crude comparisons between schools and concentration camps. With this fact in mind, here's a challenge for you. Following are five descriptions of punishment situations. Some are from actual school situations, and the other two are from less fortunate situations: one is from a Nazi prisoner of war camp, and the other is from a recent Hollywood rendition of the treatment of prisoners in chain gangs in a Southern state. The only changes in these descriptions have been to substitute words related to prisons for those related specifically to the other situations (e.g. "prisoner" for "student"). Your job is to select the three school situations.

Reader Response:

Directions: Write "S" before the three school situations.

_____ 1. The prisoner was required to kneel with arms extended and a heavy object in each hand for a half hour, while the other prisoners passed in review.

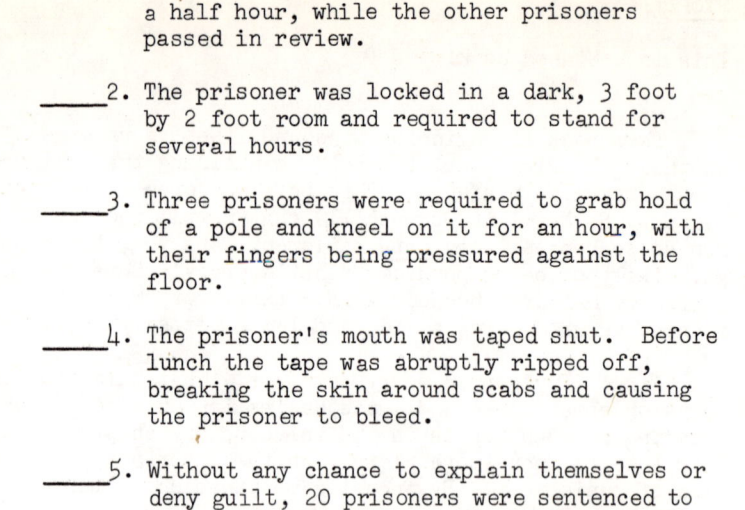

_____ 2. The prisoner was locked in a dark, 3 foot by 2 foot room and required to stand for several hours.

_____ 3. Three prisoners were required to grab hold of a pole and kneel on it for an hour, with their fingers being pressured against the floor.

_____ 4. The prisoner's mouth was taped shut. Before lunch the tape was abruptly ripped off, breaking the skin around scabs and causing the prisoner to bleed.

_____ 5. Without any chance to explain themselves or deny guilt, 20 prisoners were sentenced to three days of complete silence because of a minor violation by one of the prisoners.

Answers. Actually, the situations are all descriptions from real school situations. Nothing has been changed--these things happened to real, live students. Many of these would be considered barbaric under any circumstances, but things like this really do happen to children! Let's look at some reasons for such behavior by teachers.

AN EXPLANATION OF DRASTIC PUNISHMENT

Many of the persons who have seen the list have reacted by saying, "Those teachers were obviously sick." Some validity exists in such an evaluation. Parents and teachers are just as susceptible to pressures leading to mental disorders as anyone else. But this pressure hardly seems likely to be the whole reason for such drastic punishments.

Maybe teachers and parents resort to this type of punishment because their own teachers and parents used harsh physical punishment on them when they themselves misbehaved. This learned behavior is probably a very important factor.

Another possibility is that parents and teachers sometimes get frustrated and upset to an extreme degree and simply do things that they would never think of doing in calmer moments. When a teacher has had fifty things go wrong within a fifteen minute period, the fifty-first thing may just be more than he or she can handle. Added to this load is the fact that sometimes students back a teacher into a corner. The student humiliates the teacher, and so the teacher, who happens to be in a position of power, strikes back with force. Sometimes this action is further accentuated by colleague pressures acting upon teachers to show other teachers that he/she is as tough as any student.

    Probably the main reason why parents and teachers sometimes resort to such extreme punishments is because such punishments work! This statement is open to relatively easy refutation, for the fact could be argued that, in the long run,

"Probably the main reason why parents and teachers sometimes resort to such extreme punishments is because <u>they work</u>!"

such punishments do not work. Children may very likely stop their misbehavior only temporarily, and may immediately start planning ways to get even. As a result of the punishment children may grow up to hate school or their parents, or may behave agressively in the future. The list could be continued.

Such extreme punishments, of course, are usually employed in the midst of a very bad situation for the teacher or parent. The teacher/parent has learned either from personal experience or from watching someone else that such extreme measures are likely to bring about the immediate termination of the bad situation; and, to that extent, such punishments usually do work.

SUMMARY

The important point is, <u>PUNISHMENT WORKS</u>. When one wants to reduce or eliminate an undesirable behavior, one often can accomplish this through punishment. If punishment were necessarily cruel and harsh, as in the five examples given earlier, then such punishment could still be rejected on ethical grounds--even if it did prove effective in practice. The simple thesis of this book is that often <u>the way punishment is administered</u>, rather than the technique itself, is that which results in cruelty and/or other undesirable consequences. By isolating the essential characteristics and rejecting the inappropriate techniques, one can redeem a very useful tool for eliminating or reducing undesirable behavior.

The following Chapters discuss the effective use of punishment and how to avoid the negative side effects which often accompany punishment. In addition, other techniques are suggested to reduce undesirable behavior by developing desirable behavior which is incompatible with the inappropriate behavior. By reading these chapters, the reader can develop guidelines for deciding when punishment is appropriate, for administering punishment effectively, and--equally important--for avoiding the misuse or abuse of punishment.

Chapter **2**

THE

THREE TYPES

OF

PUNISHMENT

****

CONTENTS: The Three Types of Punishment

Unintentional Punishment

Shortcomings of Punishment

Principles of Positive Reinforcement

Guidelines for Effective Punishment

Summary

****

Objectives of Chapter 2

After reading this Chapter, you should be able to

(1) define punishment.

(2) list or identify the three types of punishment and give examples of each.

(3) list or identify the negative side effects of punishment, and give examples of each of these negative side effects.

(4) identify and give examples of the major principles of positive reinforcement.

(5) identify the guidelines for administering punishment and give examples of the implementation of these guidelines.

THE THREE TYPES OF PUNISHMENT

In this book, punishment is defined as <u>the contingent presentation of an aversive situation.</u> "Contingent" means that a person has to do something to deserve the aversive presentation. Thus, if something aversive happens to a person by sheer accident, this happening would not be defined as punishment. "Aversive" means unpleasant. An "aversive situation" occurs either when something bothersome or annoying is presented to a person or when something pleasant or desirable is taken away from a person.

Punishment can also be defined by its effects: it is a consequence which <u>reduces</u> or <u>eliminates</u> the behavior which preceded or caused it. In other words, persons prefer to avoid aversive situations and doing things which will put them in an aversive setting. Thus, the <u>only</u> use of punishment is <u>to reduce or eliminate behaviors</u>. Punishment teaches what <u>not</u> to do.

<u>Type I Punishment: Presentation of an Aversive Stimulus</u>

This type of punishment involves doing something bothersome to another person. Examples of this approach include spanking children, yelling at them, politely expressing disapproval, making children play with other children they do not like, requiring teachers to have children in their classrooms whom they cannot stand, and returning home to a spouse who drives one crazy. Note that many of these are not automatically thought of as punishments. But these situations are all unpleasant things which happen to people after performing some specific behavior. These aversive events will have the effect of discouraging the behavior which brought them about, even if this effect is unintended by the naive punisher. For example, if a teacher realizes that the reason that five "disruptive students" are in his or her class this year is because of success in dealing with one disruptive student the previous year, it is quite likely that he or she will take it easy this year to avoid having ten such students in his or her class next year. The teacher has been punished for doing a good job.

Type II Punishment: Withdrawal of a Privilege

Take something pleasant away from the person. Examples include taking away recess time, withdrawal of the use of the car on Friday night, being forced to miss one's favorite television show, and not being permitted to work on one's favorite school subject.

Type III Punishment: Addition of New Privileges, Followed by Withdrawal of These Privileges

Give the person something pleasant which was not available before, with the condition that it will be lost if a specified behavior is performed. For example, if a teenage girl does not normally have the privilege to use the family car on Friday night, she might be granted this new privilege on the condition that she will lose the privilege if she teases her little sister during the week. Or if a little boy has the unpleasant habit of tattling on his friends over trivia, he might be told that he will be permitted to play with the tape recorder for ten minutes near the end of the day, but that he will lose five minutes of that privilege for each time he tattles.

Note that a fine line exists between Type II and Type III punishment. But the simple fact is that a child who is having recess removed feels different than a child who has been promised ten minutes of extra recess and then has this extra time removed. Both children feel unpleasant; but the second child feels bad because of not getting something, whereas the first feels bad because of losing something he/she already had. Also note that a "new" privilege is new only for a reasonably short time. Thus, if you give your children an extra ten minutes of recess and continue this practice every day for six months, then contingently remove it, you are actually exercising Type II, not Type III punishment. The children are likely to view themselves as losing something rather than not getting something.

Figure 2.1 diagrams these various types of punishment. The different forms of punishment need not be pictured as dichotomous possibilities. Any given punishment might be viewed as occuring somewhere on the continuum between Type I and Type III punishment.

	Punishment	
TYPE I	TYPE II	TYPE III
Present an aversive stimulus	Take away a privilege	Add a privilege and then take it away

Examples:

Spank a child	Take away recess	Give extra recess but take it away if the child misbehaves
Yell at a child	Take away car privileges	
Express disapproval		
	Take away a toy	

Figure 2.1. Three types of punishment.

Type I punishment is defined as punishment by all writers on behavior modification theory. Type II is often referred to as "response cost." Type III is generally considered "restitution" or "frustrative nonreward." A useful technique is, however, to group all three types under the label "punishment." The main reason is that all three present an aversive situation and all are designed to eliminate or reduce behaviors. Perhaps the simplest and strongest argument in favor of classifying all three forms as punishment is illustrated by asking an adolescent girl who has just been deprived of the use of the car whether or not she is being punished. Persons being punished through Type II or III punishment often state a preference for some form of Type I punishment as being less aversive. ("You can give me twenty swats, but please let me go to football practice.")

A Short Quiz

Directions: Examine each of the following descriptions. Classify each as either Type I, II, or III punishment. (Note: These situations are not necessarily recommended forms of punishment.)

_____ 1. Making a child sit in the corner.

_____ 2. Telling a child his or her answer is wrong.

___I___ 3. Telling a person he or she is stupid.

___I___ 4. Telling a basketball player to run fifty laps for missing an easy basket.

___II___ 5. Making a child pay out of his/her own allowance for the window that he/she broke.

___III___ 6. Letting a child go to the movies unless the child fights with his/her little brother.

___I___ 7. Yelling at a child for misbehaving.

___II___ 8. Not letting two children play with a toy over which they have been fighting.

___III___ 9. Taking a child to a ball game, but leaving early when he/she starts cursing at the umpire.

Answers: 1. I   4. I   7. I
           2. I   5. I or II   8. II
           3. I   6. III   9. III

If you got one or two wrong, don't panic; think it over and figure out why you were wrong. If merely a semantic difference exists, don't worry about it. The distinctions between the three types of punishment are not always clear and can sometimes vary with your viewpoint. You may read something different into a statement than what was intended. The main factors are that you should be aware of the different possibilities and that you should have at least been able to recognize an aversive element in each of the above examples.

Sometimes more than one form of punishment is likely to occur in a given situation. For example, a teenage girl who is told she cannot go out on a date but must instead stay at home with her little brother (who is likely to persecute her all evening) is suffering from multiple forms of punishment. One need not analyze all the components of her punishment. The main point is that she has been presented with an extremely aversive situation, and she is likely to avoid doing whatever it was that got her into such a situation in the future.

Rapid Review

1. Punishment is defined as the contingent presentation of an aversive situation. "Aversive" means that the situation is _____.

2. An "aversive situation" can occur either when something __(a)_____ is <u>presented</u> to a person, or when something __(b)_____ is <u>taken away</u> from the person.

3. When an "aversive situation" occurs, this (reduces/increases) the behavior which preceded or apparently caused it.

4. The only use of punishment is to _____.

5. Spanking a child is an example of presenting an_____ _____.

6. What will spanking a child teach the child <u>to</u> do?

_____
_____
_____
_____
_____
_____
_____
_____

7. Bobby hits Sally on the head with his toy train. Mrs. Smith sees this act and takes the train away from Bobby and tells him he can't play with it for a specified period of time. This action is an example of creating an aversive situation by withdrawing a _____ stimulus.

8. What behavior is likely to decrease as a result of the withdrawal punishment?

_____
_____
_____

9. What behavior is likely to <u>increase</u> as a result of this punishment?

_____
_____

10. Susan whines when she talks. Barbara plays with Susan once in a while, and whenever she does, Barbara comes home imitating Susan. Barbara's parents have tried to keep Barbara from playing with Susan, but this is almost impossible. So Barbara's parents make a deal with their daughter: Barbara will be allowed to invite Susan over to their house to play for an hour every day, but if Barbara imitates Susan, then Barbara will not be allowed to play with Susan at all for two days. This action is an example of creating a potentially aversive situation by adding a _____ stimulus and then _____ it.

Answers: 1. Annoying (unpleasant).

2. (a) Unpleasant, annoying; (b) pleasant.

3. Reduces.

4. Reduce (or eliminate) behaviors (to teach what not to do).

5. Unpleasant (aversive) stimulus.

6. We don't know. All we know is that it will be likely to reduce the behavior which the child feels caused the spanking (assuming he/she finds the spanking to be unpleasant). The child will probably do something else instead.

7. Pleasant.

8. Hitting Sally on the head when Bobby's mother is looking.

9. We don't know. The following are some of the possibilities:

   a. Bobby might play nicely with the train.
   b. Bobby may stop playing with the train.
   c. Bobby may stop playing with Sally.
   d. Bobby may play somewhere where his mother can't see him.
   e. All of the above.

   Punishment teaches the child what not to do. Bobby will be likely to stop one specific behavior, but we can't predict what he will do instead.

10. Pleasant; removing.

UNINTENTIONAL PUNISHMENT

One of the most significant features of punishment is that the aversive situation is often brought about <u>by accident</u>. When an aversive situation occurs unintentionally, the rules of punishment still apply: The person who is punished (who has received the aversive stimulus) will avoid being punished again.

One of the most useful things that parents or teachers can gain from this book is an awareness that they often may be administering punishment <u>without even intending it</u>. If you read this book and then simply go about your work while systematically avoiding unintentional punishments, you will be doing a great service to the people with whom you deal.

<u>Examples of Accidental Punishment</u>

1. Donna cleans up her room quickly--fifteen minutes before her usual bedtime. Therefore, she is sent to bed early.

    Type II punishment: She has lost a privilege. She will be less inclined to clean up her room quickly in the future.

2. Sue comes home after a date and awakens her mother to tell her that her boyfriend has just made an improper pass at her. Her mother is at first angry about being awakened. But when she realizes that her daughter has a serious problem, she becomes quite worried and upset. Finally, she forbids Sue to be out after ten o'clock again until she is 18 years old.

    Type I punishment: Having her mother angry at being awakened was aversive to Sue.

    Type I punishment: It was also aversive to see her mother--whom she cares about--so upset.

    Type II punishment: Sue has lost a privilege of being allowed to stay out late.

    Sue will be likely to avoid all three of these aversive situations in the future. The easiest way to accomplish this avoidance will be by not discussing her problems with her mother.

3. Ms. Brown teaches sophomore English. Mrs. Johnson, the principal, puts Dirty Ralph, the meanest kid in the

school in her class. Ms. Brown views this action as a real challenge, and Dirty Ralph accomplishes more in her English class than anyone dreamed possible. The next year Mrs. Johnson assigns ten kids just like Ralph to Ms. Brown's class.

>Type I punishment: Unless some rewards are attached, Ms. Brown is likely to view this prospect as aversive. She will be likely to lose her incentive to be so successful again, since Mrs. Johnson will probably find a few more aversive stimuli somewhere if Ms. Brown leaves herself open to them.

4. Tom Billings teaches chemistry in a small college. Whenever a student asks a question, Tom has the student write a report on this question and present his or her findings to the class. The student receives no special credit for this report and is still required to do all the other work normally assigned in the course.

>Type I punishment: Tom's students will probably stop asking questions. The point is probably naive to assume that most teachers who do this are reducing questions in their courses by accident.

5. Elizabeth gets raped on her way home from work. When she reports this, it becomes a thoroughly embarrassing situation. She perceives herself as being insulted and feels that the policemen are suggesting that she actually seduced the rapist by wearing a short skirt.

>Type I punishment. Elizabeth will avoid making potentially embarrassing reports to policemen. Note that Elizabeth might be entirely inaccurate in her perceptions. The important thing is that she perceives the situation to be aversive.

Let's look at one example in greater depth.

Professor Wiley: A Detailed Example of Accidental Punishment

Professor Wiley is interested in encouraging discussion in her graduate course in educational psychology. She gives good lectures, and her students talk quite enthusiastically about the subject matter during the break in the middle of the session. The class is scheduled to meet from 6 till 9 in the evening one day a week. Dr. Wiley usually finishes her formal presentation at about 8:30 and then says, "If there are no further questions, this class will be dismissed. Are there any questions?" No one has ever asked a question

Analysis of Professor Wiley

1. The main reason students do not ask questions, even if they have some questions in their minds, is that questioning is subjected to (Type I/Type II/Type III) punishment.

2. In Type III punishment, a new privilege is added and then is contingently withdrawn. The new privilege that Professor Wiley added was (a)_____ . This privilege is contingently withdrawn if the students (b)___ _____.

3. If John Jones would ask a question, Professor Wiley would spend several minutes discussing it. Since Mr. Jones would be more interested in learning the answer to his question than in going home early, this student would not be subjected to Type III punishment, but would rather be experiencing a _____.

19

4. Even though John Jones is being positively reinforced for learning something he is interested in learning, his classmates still want to go home. John notices this, and begins to perceive a feeling of restlessness and hostility towards him. This hostility would be an example of __Type I/__ __Type II/Type III__ punishment. John would be likely to stop asking questions, even though these questions would be quite beneficial to the rest of the class.

5. Some students in the position of John Jones don't perceive the hostility of the other students. This lack of observation is often because of their extreme interest in the reward they hope to get from the answer to their questions. However, even in this case, Professor Wiley herself might be likely to perceive the hostility of the students and want to get out of the situation as soon as she can. She would be subjected to __Type I/Type II/Type III__ punishment.

Answers: 1. Type III

2. (a) Being permitted to go home a half hour early. (b) Ask questions. (This incident has been classified as Type III punishment. Note that if Professor Wiley would dismiss often enough at 8:30, the students would begin to view the class as de facto lasting from 6 until 8:30. After a few weeks, students would view being kept after 8:30 as Type II rather than Type III punishment, since the privilege of leaving at 8:30 would already belong to them and no longer be new. The students would be likely to consider staying after 8:30 to be more aversive when it is regarded as Type II punishment.)

3. Pleasant stimulus (positive reinforcer, reward).

4. Type I.

5. Type I. (If you don't believe this act, try lecturing to a group of college students who are putting on their coats.)

The best way for Professor Wiley to handle this situation would be to make sure that the students are free to ask questions without having anything to lose by doing so. A good way to do this might be to guarantee the class that the session will end at 8:45 "no matter what." If anyone is still interested in a question, Professor Wiley will stay until 9 to discuss the question with that person. The point would be best, of course, to start such a policy at the very beginning of the semester, before the students arrive at an implicit belief that the class de facto ends at 8:30.

Note that even here a strong possibility exists of accidental aversiveness. What happens if two persons ask questions? The first one asks his or her question and receives an immediate answer. Meanwhile, the second student has to endure an aversive waiting period before that student's turn comes. Instructors who follow this pattern often notice that usually only one question is asked after each class.

Example Derived From American History

According to many historians, the attitude of Great Britain towards the American colonies prior to 1763 was one of "benign neglect." For example, laws imposed taxes on certain imports and exports, but although some of these laws had been on the books for 50 to 100 years, the British seldom made any real effort to enforce them.

Around 1763, Britain was in desperate need of funds, and so turned to the colonies for help. One attempt on the part of the British to gain revenue was the passage of the Sugar Act of 1764. What this law did was to reduce the tax on molasses from sixpence to threepence, but now the law was going to be enforced. The colonists were extremely upset and reacted with violence and a boycott. The British therefore repealed the act. This type of action became a pattern: The British would pass an act, the colonists would respond with protest and/or violence, and the British would repeal the law and later impose a harsher law. Eventually both sides reached a point where they could not back down without losing face, and the American Revolution followed.

A Short Quiz

1. The Sugar Act was viewed by the colonists as (Type I/Type II/Type III) punishment.

2. For what specific action were the colonists being punished?

_____

_____

3. What did the colonists learn not to do as a result of this punishment?

_____

_____

_____

_____

4. What did the colonists learn to do as a result of this punishment?

_____

_____

_____

_____

Answers:

1. Type I. The colonists viewed themselves as de facto free from taxation. Taxes are viewed by many persons as aversive events. So the British were adding an aversive stimulus to the lives of the colonists.

2. Nobody knew. One of the worst things about the punishment from the colonists point of view was that they could see no cause for it. They were being punished for being colonists as far as they could see.

3. Stop associating too freely with the British. Don't trust the British.
The avoidance behaviors often occur when punishment is administered for a vague reason.

4. Nothing. As a result of the punishment itself, they learned nothing. The specific learning that took place was the result of the intermittent reinforcement the colonists received for their rebellious activities. Interestingly, the the British actually shaped extremely rebellious behavior. First, they reinforced the colonists for relatively minor acts of violence and protest and then for increasingly closer approximations of warlike violence. (Simultaneously, of course, other factors entered into the picture.)

SHORTCOMINGS OF PUNISHMENT

Punishment often is accompanied by serious shortcomings. In the following pages, these undesirable side effects will be discussed in detail; afterwards, suggestions will be made concerning ways to get around them. A basic premise of this book is that these shortcomings are not inherent in punishment itself, but rather occur <u>because of the manner in which punishment is administered</u> in specific situations. The shortcomings are as follows:

1. <u>Punishment only teaches what not to do</u>. Punishment does not teach the child what <u>to</u> do. The Ancient Saga tells the story of the mother and father who decided late one night that it was about time their children stopped cursing in public. The family gathered for breakfast the next morning and the oldest son initiated the conversation in his customary manner: "Pass the damn ham!" The father immediately clobbered the boy with his open hand, knocking the stunned child about twelve feet across the floor. The father then turned to the next oldest son and asked, "Now what do <u>you</u> want?" The boy was scared stiff and could only mumble, "I don't know. But I sure as hell don't want any of that damn ham!" To repeat, a major shortcoming of punishment is that, used alone, it only teaches a child what <u>not</u> to do. It does not teach what <u>to</u> do.

2. <u>Punishment often causes avoidance behaviors</u>. A person is likely to avoid both (a) the person who did the punishing if it seems that this punisher is likely to "strike again," and (b) the situation in which the person was punished if it seems that more punishment will be incurred by sticking around. Thus, in families where the father is designated as the punisher, children are likely to feel inclined to avoid the father. In schools where the assistant principal is the one whose main job seems to be to administer swats to unruly students, wise students avoid the assistant principal. Since parents and teachers are interested in teaching children appropriate behaviors, they make their job considerably more difficult if they have to make the children stop avoiding them before they can initiate instruction in appropriate behaviors.
The problem is quite similar with regard to avoidance of situations. If children are frightened of school or of staying around the house out of fear of being punished, it's going to be hard to develop adaptive skills in them.

3. **Punishment often results in a mere suppression of the undesirable behavior**. The punished person discovers that he/she had better stop doing whatever preceeded the punishment, but that the same behavior can be tried again as soon as things cool down or when the punishment becomes less probable. This shortcoming is related to the other shortcomings discussed previously. Since punishment merely teaches what not to do and suggests avoidance strategies, the punished person merely ceases the designated behavior until a time when he/she feels that the aversive situation has been successfully avoided, or a time when the pleasant results (e.g. peer attention) outweigh the aversive results (e.g. swats or detention).

4. **Punishment often results in a sort of "behavioral constriction"**. The person who is punished may discover that the safest way to avoid punishment in the future is to avoid doing anything that even remotely resembles

the punished action. Many educators argue that children approach our schools with a great deal of eagerness and creativity, and then as they go through school they are punished and told what not to do so often that they lose their spontaneity and become apathetic. The problem is one of overgeneralization: the child learns not only to avoid the specific undesirable behavior but also to avoid a large number of neutral or desirable behaviors.

5. <u>Punishment often results in undesirable modeling</u>. If the child perceives that adults solve most of their problems through punishment, that child is likely to resort to punishment to solve his/her own problems. This modeling behavior becomes especially serious when parents or teachers use such overtly aggressive tactics as spanking, hitting, and verbal abuse as their punishment techniques. In such cases parents should not be surprised when their children engage in socially undesirable behaviors such as hitting other children when the other children seem to be bothering them. The fact that the parents feel that they are "right" in administering their punishment, whereas the children are "wrong," is of little importance. What a child perceives is: "Mommy and Daddy solve their problems by hitting. I have a problem now. So I should hit the person who is responsible for my problem."

6. <u>Punishment often leads to retaliatory behavior</u>. While it is not true that every frustration must necessarily lead to some form of aggression, nevertheless the child who has been frustrated through punishment is likely to be upset. Depending on the child's level of maturity and the degree to which he/she holds the punisher responsible for the aversiveness which has been presented, the child is likely to want to get even. Many children "declare war" in this way and nurse their need for revenge for remarkably long periods of time.

7. <u>Punishment often leads to negative self evaluations</u>. A child's self concept is based on his/her self-evaluations, and these evaluations are derived, in large part, from significant others in the child's environment. If a child is constantly the recipient of punishment, he/she is likely to form a very negative self concept. Once a negative self concept is formed, the child is likely to either avoid undertaking activities out of a fear of failure or engage in undesirable activities which are related to this negative self evaluation.

Summary of Shortcomings

If these shortcomings of punishment were inevitable, perhaps punishment should never be used as a behavior control technique. The author's view in this book, however, is that such negative side effects are not actually inevitable. These shortcomings are not inherent in the act of punishment itself, but rather they result from the way punishment is administered. If punishment is properly administered, these undesirable consequences can be minimized or eliminated entirely.

Two things need to be re-emphasized:

1. Punishment is an extremely useful technique to teach a person what not to do. This will often be your goal.

2. Punishment is very frequently poorly administered. Therefore, the undesirable side effects occur very frequently.

With these two factors in mind, the fact seems apparent that a person who does not administer punishment appropriately is faced with two equally undesirable alternatives:

1. Rejecting a very useful technique.

2. Imposing these undesirable consequences upon the person to be punished.

Therefore, it is extremely important to become proficient in the use of punishment. This proficiency does not mean that you should punish children as often as possible or brag about new and unique ways you have devised to torture children. Nor does this proficiency mean that you should resort to punishment first whenever a problem arises. What proficiency in punishment does mean is that when punishment is the appropriate technique (which will sometimes be the case) you will be able to punish appropriately. You want to be sure you will accomplish the desired goal, rather than some unexpected goal.

PRINCIPLES OF POSITIVE REINFORCEMENT

At this point discussing some of the principles of positive reinforcement is useful. Positive reinforcement is extremely important: it should be the main behavior-control strategy of parents and teachers. The fact that the discussion of positive reinforcement is confined to a small part of one Chapter should not be taken as a suggestion that it is unimportant. Quite the contrary, positive reinforcement should be used to solve perhaps 90 to 95 percent of all behavior problems. The reason the discussion is limited here is because this is a book about punishment, not about behavior control in general.

Positive reinforcement is defined as the contingent delivery of a pleasant stimulus. This technique causes the behavior after which it is administered to increase. The important consideration is that the stimulus (reward) has to be viewed by the recipient as pleasant. Thus, what is positively reinforcing for one individual at one time may not be positively reinforcing to that same individual at another time or to another individual at any time. In Table 2.1 (p. 27) listed a large number of things which are sometimes positively reinforcing. This list is not meant to be conclusive or comprehensive, but rather to show the large variety of things which can be positively reinforcing.

Table 2.1 Some Examples of Positive Reinforcement

candy	praise
money	stars for good papers
movies	beer and pretzels
thank-you notes	watching television
success on crossword puzzle	watching your enemy fail at something
playing baseball	toys
watching baseball	doing enjoyable schoolwork
losing weight	helping teacher
sleeping late	kisses and hugs
passing English 101	trading stamps
interesting conversation	good books
sunset	invigorating walks
promotion	beating up a bully

Intrinsic or Extrinsic Positive Reinforcement

Positive reinforcement can be either intrinsic or extrinsic. Intrinsic reinforcers are those where the delivery of the pleasant stimulus occurs primarily inside the recipient; for example, pride in one's work or the satisfaction inherent in discovering the answer to a bewildering question. If this book helps you formulate useful strategies for dealing with your children, the book is probably intrinsically reinforcing for you to read. Extrinsic reinforcement, on the other hand, refers to the delivery of an external pleasant stimulus, such as money, praise from a teacher, or candy. If you are reading this book to obtain a grade in a course, then it is extrinsically reinforcing for you to read it. Of course, something can be under the simultaneous influence of both extrinsic and intrinsic reinforcement; for example, you could be reading this book for both of the previous reasons.

Intrinsic vs. Extrinsic Reinforcers

Many parents and teachers resent the idea of using extrinsic reinforcers, suggesting that children are to do certain things just because they are appropriate things to do. "A child should not have to be bribed to do everything." This attitude holds a great amount of truth for it is highly undesirable to maintain behaviors entirely through external reinforcement. The eventual goal should always involve intrinsic maintenance of the behaviors. Look at these two examples:

Example of the Misuse of Extrinsic Reinforcement:

Mr. Jefferson teaches freshman mathematics. His students show no inclination to learn. The students see no relevance of anything he teaches to real life. To keep the students quiet, Mr. Jefferson makes the following deal with them. If the students work quietly and pay attention during the first 45 minutes of each class hour, they can have the last fifteen minutes free to study other subjects or to talk quietly. The students like this idea and stop being rowdy. The classroom becomes remarkably quiet during the first 45 minutes and Mr. Jefferson is able to teach in peace.

Example of Correct Use of Extrinsic Reinforcement:

Mr. Brown teaches freshman mathematics. His students also show no inclination to learn. However, he teaches math in such a way that it is in fact directly applicable to real life--the problem is that none of the students have ever paid enough attention to find out that the course is meaningful. Mr. Brown makes the same deal that Mr. Jefferson made with his students, and the results are the same. Mr. Brown is then permitted to present his information in a quiet atmosphere.

Mr. Jefferson is depending entirely on extrinsic reinforcement. He is simply bribing the students to be quiet. If the bribe is removed, the students are quite likely to return to their previous rowdy behavior. Mr. Brown, on the other hand, is using an extrinsic reinforcer as a starter stimulus to make the more intrinsic reinforcer (his useful math class) available to the students. If Mr. Brown has to withdraw his external reinforcer, it's likely that at least some of the students would still be intrinsically motivated to learn math. Mr. Brown is using an effective behavior modification program: he has built in a plan to transfer an extrinsic reinforcer to intrinsic motivation. Tactics such as those applied by Mr. Jefferson are sometimes perhaps necessary, but Mr. Brown's course of action is preferable.

Here's another example dealing with a younger child.

Example: Colleen--Another School Example

Colleen is a second grader who absolutely hates school work. She refuses to do her arithmetic. No threats or praise from her teacher can get her started on arithmetic. Finally, her teacher, Ms. Jones, makes a deal with her. If Colleen does one arithmetic problem, she can have a piece of candy. Colleen does the problem and receives the candy. As she gives Colleen the candy, the teacher says, "That was very good work Colleen" and grins happily. Colleen suggests that she would like another piece of candy, and the teacher negotiates another deal, each time praising Colleen and smiling as she presents the candy. Eventually Ms. Jones gives candy only at the completion of a page or a unit, but she continues to smile and praise much in between.

Colleen has started out working only for a primary reinforcer (extrinsic reinforcer), candy. Eventually, through constant pairing with the primary reinforcer, praise and smiles from the teacher also become positively reinforcing. These are secondary reinforcers (intrinsic reinforcers). Hopefully, Colleen will eventually work for praise alone, with only an occasional extrinsic or primary reinforcer. Eventually she might even finish a task, look at it, and say to herself, "That's really a good job." Colleen would thus have made the entire transfer to intrinsic reinforcement. If this transfer does not happen automatically, the teacher can facilitate such transfer by saying such things as "What do I usually say to you when you do a job like that?" as she delivers her own extrinsic reinforcers.

Social Reinforcement

Another frequently used term is social reinforcement, which refers to a pleasant stimulus which arises out of a social situation. Being allowed to attend a party, praise, and peer prestige are examples of social reinforcement. Social reinforcers are secondary, not primary, reinforcers, and as such they have to be learned by the child. Some children learn the value of these reinforcers almost automatically, while others require systematic instruction, as in the case of Colleen. Social reinforcers can be extremely strong sources of reinforcement for young children. Often a child is receiving social reinforcement from his or her peers for behaviors which are incompatible with behaviors the parent or teacher is trying to develop.

Token Reinforcement

Another important term is token reinforcement, which refers to providing the recipient with a "token" reward at the completion of a desired behavior, with the understanding that the token can be turned in for a "back-up" reinforcer later on. The token reinforcer can be a mark on a piece of paper, a bingo token, a gold star, or anything which symbolizes achievement and progress toward some goal. The main advantages of token reinforcement are that tokens can be delivered almost immediately after the performance of the desired behavior and that many persons in the same group can be working toward entirely different goals or back-up reinforcers at the same time. The disadvantage is that the child has to be capable of delaying gratification long enough to wait for the back-up reinforcer.

"Shaping" in Positive Reinforcement

One of the most important ideas in positive reinforcement is that of "shaping." This reinforcement refers to the strategy of reinforcing behaviors which are short of the desired outcome, but which are steps in the right direction. For example, if a child has not spoken in class all year, shaping might suggest reinforcing that child for looking at you or giving a one-word answer. If you wait for the final outcome behavior (speaking in front of the whole class) you might never get a chance to do any reinforcing. An important characteristic of shaping is that it enables the child to get reinforced quite often and to develop a sort of "success syndrome." If, on the other hand, the child has to wait until he or she can do the whole desired project correctly before getting a reinforcer, that child is much more likely to view himself or herself as an incompetent failure and give up trying.

Modeling and Vicarious Reinforcement

<u>Modeling</u> and <u>vicarious reinforcement</u> often are employed in connection with positive reinforcement programs. In modeling someone acts as a "model" and demonstrates the outcome behavior to the learner. In everyday situations modeling is how children learn most of their behaviors, and it is possible to systematically provide models to teach specific behaviors. The model is more likely to be imitated if (a) he or she is <u>similar</u> to the learner, (b) the model has a certain amount of <u>prestige</u> in the eyes of the learner, and (c) the desirable behavior is demonstrated in a way which is easily observable and duplicated by the learner.

Example: Marc--A Childhood Example

Marc was two years old and needed his first haircut. His mother decided to use positive reinforcement. She planned that she would start to cut his hair and then praise him with "What a big boy you are!" every time she snipped his hair. The problem was that as soon as Marc saw the scissors, he started screaming hysterically, and the only way he got his haircut was when his father got him in a half nelson and held him while his mother cut his hair. Two months later it came time to try again. This time Marc's mother gave his Daddy a haircut first. His Daddy hammed it up and demonstrated great joy in the beautification process which was taking place. As soon as Daddy was finished, he took the cloth off himself, put it on Marc, and said, "Now it's your turn." Marc sat there quietly, and after the first snip the mother was able to proceed with her "What a big boy!" program as originally planned.

Reinforcing the model (vicarious reinforcement) has the same
effect as reinforcing the learner. Thus, when Marc saw his
Daddy taking obvious delight in getting his haircut, this
delight was vicariously reinforcing to him and increased the
probability that he would sit quietly. Another frequent
example of the use of vicarious reinforcement is to ignore a
child who is not ready for reading class and to praise the
child next to him or her for being ready. The first child
often will get his or her book out quite quickly.

The "Reinforcement Schedule"

The "schedule" of reinforcement refers to how frequently
the reinforcer is given. In an extinction schedule, the
reinforcer is not given at all, and this will cause the undesirable behavior to decrease. With a continuous schedule the
reinforcer is administered for every correct performance of
the desired behavior. Continuous reinforcement is a good
schedule to use to cause a very rapid development of a new
behavior. With an intermittent schedule the reinforcer is

administered on a less consistent basis, either irregularly or after more than one correct response has been performed. When behavior learned through continuous reinforcement is exposed to an extinction schedule, the behavior is eliminated very rapidly. On the other hand, when behavior learned through an intermittent schedule is submitted to an extinction schedule, the behavior persists for a longer time before it is eliminated. When developing new behaviors, therefore, a good idea is to start with a continuous reinforcement schedule and then switch to an intermittent reinforcement schedule once the behavior is learned. This reinforcement schedule transition will result in both rapid learning and long retention.

Summary of Positive Reinforcement

Positive reinforcement is desirable. Introductory material has been presented with explanation of the frequently used terms. For more comprehensive coverage the reader is referred to books listed in the annotated Bibliography.

In this section only those terms have been included which are needed to understand this book and to help the reader integrate the concept of positive reinforcement with the material discussed in this book. The author intends for this book to fill a specific void. Other books do an extremely good job at providing information on how to develop new behaviors, but give minimal attention to how to eliminate behaviors. This author feels that the elimination of behaviors is a legitimate and very important concern of parents and teachers, and for that purpose has written this book. At the same time the author wants to stress that a parent or teacher who knows <u>only</u> how to eliminate behaviors is going to have a very impoverished learning program for his or her children or students. In reality, you should spend more time developing desirable behaviors than eliminating undesirable ones. Therefore, you should attempt to learn about positive reinforcement--much more than is contained in these few pages.

GUIDELINES FOR EFFECTIVE PUNISHMENT

The following guidelines will be helpful in making punishment work effectively:

1. <u>Punish a behavior, not a person</u>. Punishment should never be presented or perceived as a personal attack. There is little point in telling a person that he is a "bad boy" or a "spoiled brat."

    <u>Examples</u>: If two children are preparing to hit each other with baseball bats, this act might be a good occasion for punishment, since hitting with

bats is something <u>not</u> to do. Some bad ways to present the punishment would be: "Can't you two ever stop fighting?" "You could kill each other with those bats!" "What the hell are you trying to do?" Some better approaches might be: "Bats are for hitting baseballs, not baseball players. I'm going to take the bats away for today." "When fights start it's best to cool off for a while. You sit over there and you sit on the other side line. You can rejoin the game as soon as you've cooled off."

<u>Reader Response</u>

Directions: Try a couple yourself. Reword each of these statements in the space provided.

Situations:

1. (To a child who has not finished his/her math assignment within the required period.) "I'll teach you not to be so lazy. You'll stay in during recess until you get busy and work!"

_____

_____

_____

_____

2. (To an adolescent who has stayed out two hours beyond curfew.) "If you don't have the sense of responsibility to come home on time, you're not going anywhere any more. You're grounded for a month."

_____

_____

_____

_____

<u>Sample Answers</u>:

1. "This work isn't finished yet. You'll have to stay in during recess to finish it."

2. "It really makes us worry, Son, when you stay out late and we don't know where you are. You'll have to stay home evenings until we know this won't happen again."

Problems Arising From A Personal Attack

An obvious problem with the personal attack instead of the impersonal punishment is that it puts the person being punished on the defensive side of an argument. A second problem is that the personal attack attaches a label. Once a person is labeled "lazy" or "irresponsible" he/she is provided with a rationale for adopting that role; and, adopting the role may often be easier and more rewarding than working to reject or disprove the label.

Be sure that the child understands that you think he/she is really a fine, lovable person, even though the action the child just performed is inappropriate. This positive regard is something that should be conveyed in an overall relationship with a child rather than in a single sentence just prior to the administration of punishment. In other words, it's not very useful to say, "John, you're a fine lovable person, but you just threw a spitwad and will therefore have to go to the time-out area." The best response is to let John know that you think highly of him by the way you treat him before and after the punishment. A good idea is to arrange a chance for John to perform some desirable act shortly after punishment so that you can again express your high regard for him and demonstrate that he has not gone down in your overall esteem.

Situation:

Danny usually plays very nicely with his friends. He is now three years old, and is starting to imitate some rather selfish behaviors which some of the older children in the neighborhood exhibit. Danny's mother has told him that she wants him to be like "Danny," not like the other children, and that if he grabs toys from little children, he'll have to stay in the house. One day she sees Danny grabbing a toy from the two-year-old next door. She says, "Danny, those are Ronald's toys. Don't take them from him like that. Now you'll have to stay in the house for a while." Fifteen minutes later she tells Danny to come outside and adds, "You're a good boy. Let's read your favorite storybook together."

Is this last sentence a good way to demonstrate to Danny that he has his mother's overall approval in spite of the fact that it was necessary to punish him?

_____ Yes

_____ No

_____
_____
_____
_____

Sample Answer:

    This was a hard one! No. The approach would have been more constructive to first give Danny an opportunity to do something desirable and then give him the reward in the context of his desirable behavior. He would then know he was good because he had just done something good (as opposed to his previous bad behavior) and his mother had rewarded him for it.

2. Specify the behavior that is being punished. The child should not be left with a "What did I do now?" feeling. If the child knows exactly what was done to incur the punishment and wants to avoid the punishment in the future, such avoidance can be achieved most efficiently if he/she can quickly focus on the specified behavior. A related problem is that if the undesired behavior is not delineated carefully enough, the child is likely to avoid more behaviors than you really want the child to avoid. To illustrate, if a little girl is punished for laughing uproariously while another student is talking to the class she might stop her spontaneous laughter on the playground if she overgeneralizes the punishment. The appropriate course of action would be to teach the discrimination by pointing out that loud laughter in the classroom makes it hard for the teacher and the other students to concentrate. The teacher might later want to make specific efforts to praise the child on the playground for making a funny remark and using her high spirits in an appropriate fashion.

Example:

    A notorious example of overgeneralized punishment is cited by educators who maintain that school systematically eliminates creativity in children. Being informed that they are wrong is viewed as at least mildly aversive by most children and adults just as being informed that they are right is at least mildly reinforcing). When children give wrong answers and are told they are wrong, they are likely to attempt to stop the behavior which leads to being told they are wrong. However, many of them feel that they are being punished for "giving it a try" or for offering an hypothesis, rather than for a misuse of a cognitive process or a simple mistake in memory. This fact is especially true if the punishment is severe (e.g. being called wrong in front of all their peers). When this punishment happens, the child can avoid being called wrong in the future by simply not volunteering and not trying very hard. (The situation is less aversive to be called wrong if you haven't even tried than if you have given your best efforts only to fail.) In this instance an appropriate action would be to help the child discriminate between situations which have a simple right or wrong answer (addition, spelling) and those where the process of generating a creative hypothesis is more important. The child should then be rewarded rather than punished for generating a reasonable hypothesis.

With children who are extremely likely to overgeneralize negative feedback, the best action is to go to extremes to minimize such negative feedback. For example, when a child looks at "4 + 3" and says "9," rather than saying "Wrong," simply say "7" and go on to the next problem. Note that this overgeneralization is an extreme case. Most children are able to accept "No" or "Wrong" as simple feedback. But teachers should be aware that, especially among children who feel insecure, the alternative approach might be useful.

The important fact is that teachers should be cautious to avoid having children view themselves as being punished for trying to solve problems. If children perceive this to be the case, they are likely to stop trying.

Note that in many cases the child will be able to recognize the specific undesirable behavior without a detailed explanation by the parent or teacher. A sermon need not accompany every punishment. What is important is that the parent or teacher be aware that the child might not understand exactly for what he or she is being punished. If this misunderstanding is the case, then further specification is in order.

3. <u>Punish as early as possible in the behavioral sequence</u>.
   If you see John reaching for Sally's purse (which he usually throws in the waste basket), punish him at that point. (Be certain, of course, that throwing the purse in the wastebasket is what John really intends

to do.) If you wait until the purse bangs into the corner waste basket, then your punishment has to compete with the rewards he reaps from Sally's screams and the class's uproarious applause. To outweigh such positive reinforcements, you would have to resort to a much more severe punishment than if you had punished early in the sequence.

4. <u>Match the severity of the punishment to the severity of the misbehavior.</u> This matching is actually harder than it sounds, because either the punisher or the recipient of the punishment is likely to make an inaccurate estimate of the severity of either the misbehavior or the punishment. If the punishment is too light, the reinforcers inherent in the undesired behavior are likely to outweigh the punishment. If the punishment is too severe, the child is likely to engage in avoidance, suppressive, self-devaluative or retaliatory behaviors.

"Well, Eddy, I'm sorry, but since you didn't finish your math assignment, you'll just have to stay after school with me and finish it here."

(Be certain that the child views the punishment as aversive!)

5. <u>Be sure that the child views the punishment as aversive</u>. Something is aversive and therefore an effective punisher to a child not because <u>we</u> think it is aversive, but rather because the <u>child</u> perceives it as aversive. What is punishment to one child in one situation may not be punishing to that same child in a different situation or to another child in any situation. Many of the things we think are aversive to children and students are actually positively reinforcing to them!

Examples:

Rick is a football player. Whenever he talks out of turn in history class, he is required to come to the front of the room and receive three hard swats from a powerfully-built teacher with a very thick paddle. The swats hurt a little, but no more than a solid block on the football field. Rick happens to know that one of his friends is keeping a list of the number of swats he receives. If he gets 35 more within the next ten days, he'll break the school record. (Rick is being positively reinforced by peer admiration.)

Eddie is required to sit in the corner whenever he misbehaves. The corner is right next to the bed, and he keeps a supply of comic books hidden under the mattress.

Sandi is kept after school for detention almost every night. Paula also spends much time on detention, almost always on the same nights with Sandi. Sandi's parents don't approve of Paula, and this is the only time they can get together. The two girls later get a ride home from school with Paula's boyfriend.

The opposite is also true: many things that teachers think are positively reinforcing actually are viewed as punishment by children. For example, when a sixth-grade boy helps a sixth-grade girl put her coat on, the teacher might think that it is positive reinforcement to say in front of the whole class, "Why Johnny, that's the nicest thing I've ever seen you do!" But Johnny is likely to view such a remark as a source of peer embarrassment. The next worse thing would have been if the teacher would have said "cutest" instead of "nicest."

6. <u>Whenever possible, use punishment in conjunction with the reinforcement of an alternative behavior</u>. This way you will be teaching what <u>to</u> do, as well as what <u>not</u> to do.

7. <u>Whenever possible, use non-punitive forms of punishment</u>. This form will often, though not always, suggest using Type II and Type III punishment.

SUMMARY

Punishment has been defined as the contingent presentation of an aversive situation. Three conceptually distinct ways to bring about an aversive situation have been defined as the three "types" of punishment. Type I punishment involves the contingent presentation of an aversive stimulus; for example, spanking a child or doing something to bother the child. Type II punishment involves the contingent removal of something pleasant; for example, the removal of driving privileges for breaking traffic laws. Type III punishment involves the addition of a new privilege and then the contingent removal of this new privilege. All three types of punishment can occur by accident as well as intentionally; and the effects are exactly the same whether the punishment occurs intentionally or accidentally.

One reason to avoid the use of punishment is that punishment often is accompanied by negative side effects--shortcomings which can actually do harm beyond what we intend for the recipient of the punishment. This author argues, however, that these negative side effects occur because of the way punishment is administered and are not automatically inherent in the act of punishment itself. Punishment is a very useful technique for teaching what <u>NOT</u> to do, and the effective use of punishment is strongly recommended in situations when such teaching, "what <u>not</u> to do," is the goal of the parent or teacher.

Chapter **3**

NEGATIVE REINFORCEMENT -- GETTING RELIEF

****

CONTENTS: Factors Influencing the Effectiveness of Negative Reinforcement

Case Illustrations

Accidental Negative Reinforcement

Occasions for Negative Reinforcement

Summary

****

Objectives of Chapter 3

After reading this Chapter, one should be able to

(1) define and give examples of negative reinforcment.

(2) identify the factors which influence the effectiveness of negative reinforcement.

(3) identify examples of accidental improper use of negative reinforcement.

(4) identify occasions when negative reinforcement is possible and appropriate.

The presentation of an aversive situation has the effect of reducing the behavior it follows, and this action has been referred to as punishment. Once an aversive situation is present, however, the fact should be obvious that the removal of this unpleasantness should have some effect on behavior. As a matter of fact, the removal of an aversive situation has the effect of increasing the behavior it follows, and this is referred to as negative reinforcement. The following diagram might be helpful.

Aversive Situation	Pleasant Stimulus	Unpleasant Stimulus
Contingently Given	POSITIVE REINFORCEMENT (REWARD)	PUNISHMENT
Contingently Removed	PUNISHMENT	NEGATIVE REINFORCEMENT

The diagram can easily be understood if you imagine yourself eating some food. If you eat the food and then feel good because of it, a pleasant stimulus is contingently given; and therefore you'll be likely to eat that food again. If you eat the food and therefore feel bad (unpleasant stimulus contingently given), you'll be unlikely to eat the food again, because you have been punished. If you're feeling really good and the good feeling goes away completely as soon as you eat the food (pleasant stimulus contingently removed), you'll likewise be less likely to eat it in the future, since you've been punished for eating the particular food. This situation now leaves the last possibility. If you're feeling bad and eat something that takes the bad feeling away, will your eating behavior be reinforced in the future or not? Of course your eating behavior will be reinforced. Your eating of that food will be strengthened (reinforced) in the future. Since this reinforcement occurs in a negative way (by having something unpleasant removed, as opposed to having something added), this form of reinforcement is referred to as <u>negative reinforcement</u>.

Both forms of punishment result in a reduction of the behavior. Both forms of reinforcement result in an increase in the behavior. Positive reinforcement is "positive" in the sense that the reinforcement results from something being <u>added</u>. Negative reinforcement is "negative" in the sense that the reinforcement results from something being <u>removed</u>.

An example from animal psychology might prove useful. If an experimenter wants to teach a rat to push a lever, two ways are equally effective to accomplish this training. The experimenter could give the rat a pellet of its favorite food every time the lever is pressed or the experimenter could wire the floor of the cage with electricity and then turn the shocks off for a few seconds every time the rat happens to press the lever. To the extent that the rat either wants the food badly or is extremely bothered by the electrical shocks, the rat will work harder; and to the extent that the rat is not hungry or is not troubled by the shocks the rat will tend to slack off his behavior.

Human experience offers numerous examples of learning by negative reinforcement. We have learned to scratch mosquito bites. Why? Because an aversive situation (itching) is immediately removed contingent upon scratching. We wear coats and hats in cold weather because we have learned that this apparel gets us away from the aversiveness of the bitter cold. We take aspirin because it gives us relief from the aversiveness of a nagging headache. People spank their children because they are relieved from the aversiveness of the children's obnoxious behavior.

I have found that most of my students have an irresistible urge to say "negative reinforcement" when they mean "punishment." This usage is unfortunate, for this usage distorts or misrepresents a useful concept--that of strengthening a behavior by terminating aversiveness. Just remember: when we <u>reinforce</u> a behavior, we <u>strengthen</u> it. We can strengthen the behavior in two ways: by <u>adding</u> something pleasant (positive reinforcement) or by <u>giving relief</u> from something unpleasant (negative reinforcement). Getting relief strengthens a behavior--whether the relief is from a mosquito bite, from cold weather, from a nagging headache, or from sitting in the corner.

Also note that two ways exist for getting relief from an aversive situation. One way is to <u>avoid</u> the aversive situation in the first place. Wearing warm clothes and staying away from a nagging spouse are examples of this type of negative

44

reinforcement. The second way is to <u>escape</u> from the aversiveness once it is present. Scratching a mosquito bite, taking an aspirin for a headache, and hitting another child to get that child to be quiet are examples of such escape. Other things being equal, a person is likely to be more strongly motivated to get relief (seek negative reinforcement) when a need to escape is present than when the need is merely to avoid a future state of aversiveness. Thus a person is more motivated to scratch the mosquito bite than to avoid the mosquitoes in the first place. Likewise, people are more likely to take an aspirin when they have a hangover than to avoid getting the hangover, even if they know the hangover is coming. This phenomenon occurs largely because positive reinforcers are competing with the negative reinforcers when we consider the <u>avoidance</u> behaviors, whereas the need for negative reinforcement is more predominant when we consider the <u>escape</u> behaviors (i.e. the aversiveness is already present when we are seeking escape behaviors). This fact will be important to keep in mind when discussing negative reinforcement in conjunction with punishment. Some punishments (such as spanking or ridicule) can be prevented only by avoidance behaviors--no opportunity exists to learn-whereas other punishments (such as time-out) provide an opportunity to learn from escape behaviors as well as from avoidance behaviors. This point will become clear in the discussion of corporal punishment in Chapter 5.

RAPID REVIEW

1. The presentation of an aversive situation to a person has been referred to as _____.

2. Punishment has the effect of (<u>increasing/decreasing</u>) the behavior which it immediately follows.

3. The aversive situation which has been referred to as punishment can consist of either the (a) _____ of an unpleasant stimulus or the (b) _____ of a pleasant stimulus.

4. Once an aversive situation is present, its removal also has an effect. The removal of an aversive situation has the effect of increasing the behavior which immediately proceeded the removal of the aversiveness. This strengthening of behavior resulting from the removal of an aversive situation is referred to as negative reinforcement. Negative reinforcement has the effect of (<u>increasing/ decreasing</u>) the behavior which it follows.

5. The effects of punishment and negative reinforcement are (<u>identical/opposite</u>).

6. The effects of <u>positive reinforcement</u> and <u>negative reinforcement</u> are (identical/opposite).

7. The occurence of an aversive situation is likely to have two separate effects. When the aversive situation is <u>presented</u> to a person, the person views this as (a)_____ and this is likely to (increase/decrease) the behavior the person was performing just before the presentation of the aversive situation. When the aversive situation is <u>removed</u>, the person views this as (b)_____, and this is likely to (increase/decrease) the behavior which immediately preceded the removal of the aversive situation.

Answers:
1. Punishment.
2. Decreasing.
3. (a) Presentation; (b) Elimination (removal).
4. Increasing.
5. Opposite.
6. Identical.
7. (a) Unpleasant, decrease; (b) Pleasant, increase.

FACTORS INFLUENCING THE EFFECTIVENESS OF NEGATIVE REINFORCEMENT

The effectiveness of negative reinforcement is subject to many of the same considerations as positive reinforcement.

1. <u>The negative reinforcer has to be perceived as reinforcing by the recipient</u>. What is negatively reinforcing to one child may not be reinforcing to another child. What is negatively reinforcing to a child on one specific occasion may be non-reinforcing to the same child on a different occasion.

2. <u>The negative reinforcement should occur as soon as possible after the occurrence of the desired behavior</u>. For this reason, reinforcers which occur automatically upon the performance of a behavior are quite efficient. On occasions when it is necessary to delay the reinforcement, verbal reconstruction of the original situation is a useful substitute. (For example, "Remember that test we took last Friday? Well, you got a 95 on it, and so you won't have to spend your free periods studying with me this week. Keep up the good work.")

3. <u>The negative reinforcer should be logically related to the behavior which has been performed</u>.

4. <u>Negative reinforcement is effective to the extent that it is contingent upon the performance of a specific behavior.</u> Just as positive reinforcers such as candy, money, and praise are ineffective if they are administered every day at 3:00, so also, the removal of a punishment at the mere expiration of a time limit will reinforce no desirable behavior.

5. <u>Negative reinforcement can and often should be used in conjunction with other behavior control techniques.</u>

6. <u>Negative reinforcement is just as likely as positive reinforcement or punishment to remain merely an external control technique.</u> A reinforcement program should be designed to transfer to <u>internal</u> control in the learner. This transfer will occur more readily if the activity for which the learner is being negatively reinforced has some intrinsic usefulness and if the learner is aware of this intrinsic usefulness. Thus systematic external negative reinforcement should be a temporary technique to bring the learner into contact with intrinsic reinforcers which he/she would otherwise never encounter.

Another important factor is that whenever aversive conditions are contingently manipulated, <u>undesirable side effects</u> are likely to occur. Thus awareness of and control for such factors as reduction of spontaneity, avoidance behaviors, and undersirable modeling of aggressive behaviors become necessary. (These problems are more fully discussed in Chapter 2.) When using negative reinforcement, a simple but important decision must be made: Do I really want to run the risk of these side effects? If the risk of side effects is minimal or if the behavior to be taught is important and can be taught much more efficiently through negative reinforcement, then negative reinforcement will be the technique of choice. Otherwise, another technique may be in order.

CASE ILLUSTRATIONS

<u>Carl: A Family Example</u>

Nick and Betty wanted to take their $2\frac{1}{2}$ year old son Carl for short walks in the evening. They often found this walk to be a very frustrating experience, however, because Carl had the bad habit of sitting down or dawdling in the middle of the street whenever they came to one. This often was dangerous. They could have solved the problem by simply picking Carl up and carrying him whenever they came to a street, but they preferred not to do this. For one thing, carrying Carl would be a hassle, and for another thing, it wouldn't teach Carl to cross the street by himself, an important concept if they ever wanted to take him along on a walk when they had their arms full. Every evening for two weeks they took Carl for a walk. The rules: "Whenever we come to a street, you have to hold Mommy and Daddy's hand until we reach the other side and then you can let go." When they approached a street, Nick would grab one hand and Betty the other. They then would start to cross the street at a normal pace. If Carl would start to sit down or to slow down excessively, Nick and Betty simply continued at the same pace. The result was that Carl's feet were dragged very slightly. If Carl would start to move his feet to walk in a normal fashion, the dragging would stop. Since the dragging annoyed Carl, he very quickly learned to move his feet and to walk across the street without delays. During the second week a surprise result came up. When they came to the first street, Carl said, "I can cross by myself." Nick and Betty immediately agreed that if Carl would walk right next to one of them, he could cross by himself; but if he lagged behind, they would have to hold his hand. By the end of the second week Carl was almost always crossing by himself, and whenever he failed, Nick and Betty would simply revert to the old rules.

Analysis of Carl:

1. The slight dragging of Carl's feet was a **punishment** (Type I). The effectiveness of this punishment probably was increased because it occurred automatically (and therefore immediately) whenever the undesirable behavior occurred. The punishment also appeared as a logical outcome and would be likely to have few undesirable side effects, such as hatred for the punisher. Such side effects would have become increasingly probable if the dragging would have been harshly administered.

2. As soon as Carl started to move his feet, he was **negatively reinforced** for walking. This reinforcement was automatic, immediate, and appeared as a logical outcome.

3. Having his hand held by his parents also was viewed as a **punishment** (Type I) by Carl. Adults often fail to realize that requiring a child to walk with his hand extended above his head is a very difficult task, and therefore aversive. Though accidental, this punishment probably was effective because it was almost automatic and appeared to Carl to be logically related to the task of getting across the street. The confinement of free movement was punishing also.

4. Being allowed to walk across the street without having his hand held was **negatively reinforcing** for Carl, since he was getting out of the aversive situation of having his hand extended over his head and his freedom confined. This negative reinforcement was quite effective because it occurred automatically and was logically related to the task.

5. Carl's walking behavior was probably being **positively reinforced** by the intrinsic satisfaction of being a "big boy," as well as by any words of praise from his parents. If Carl really enjoyed the walks, they should say things to him like, "Now that you can cross streets so well, we can go on a lot of walks, can't we?" Since walking is incompatible with sitting and dawdling, these positive reinforcers actually serve to reduce the undesirable behaviors. (This technique will be discussed in greater detail in the next Chapter.)

6. Note that Carl's original misbehavior would be considered by many to be a serious problem, requiring rather firm measures. Many parents rightly argue that if their child plays in the street, the best way to respond is by spanking the child "to teach him/her

never to do it again." Since getting hit by a car a single time may be one time too many, the parents would be willing to risk a few undesirable consequences to get their point across most efficiently. Carl's parents, however, selected a much milder form of punishment. They were able to do so because they had control over the situation. Had they responded with a harsher punishment (such as spanking), undesirable side effects would have been much more likely to occur--most notably, Carl might have developed a distaste for walks. In addition, spanking would have minimized the opportunity for their effective use of negative reinforcement, since it would have been difficult to terminate the spanking immediately upon the performance of the desired behavior.

Ronnie: A School Example

Ronnie was a fifth grader who rarely completed even half of her math problems by the time everybody else in the class was finished with theirs. Her teacher noticed that Ronnie especially liked the art hour which immediately followed the math period. She was fairly certain that Ronnie's delay in finishing her work was the result of unwillingness rather than deficits in the particular skills, so she established some rules for Ronnie: Ronnie would not be allowed to start on her art work until she finished her math assignment. The first day, Ronnie followed her usual pattern of not finishing on time, so the teacher told her that she would have to complete the math assignment before she could start on art. Ronnie obviously was upset, but the teacher was quite happy when within ten minutes Ronnie turned in the completed assignment. Ronnie was permitted to start on her art work, but the teacher's happiness diminished considerably when she discovered that Ronnie had gotten over half of the answers wrong. The results were similar the next day. On the third day, the teacher changed the rule: Ronnie would have to finish the assignment with no more than three errors before starting her art work. That day Ronnie completed the assignment within the math period, but she missed fifteen problems. She was given a second assignment, but she didn't finish that one, even by the end of art period. The next day she worked much more slowly, and completed the assignment on time with only two errors. After a week of this, the teacher said that she would no longer check the paper immediately. If Ronnie turned in a completed assignment on time, she would be allowed to start her art work; but if the teacher found more than three mistakes that evening, the rules would be reinstated starting the next day for another week. There were no further problems, and after two more weeks the rules were dropped altogether.

Analysis of Ronnie:

1. When Ronnie failed to complete her math assignment, she was not permitted to start on her art work. This example is of Type (Type I, II, or III) punishment.

2. This type of punishment is designed to (increase/decrease) Ronnie's behavior of excessive slowness in completing assignments.

3. What behavior does this type of punishment increase?

4. As soon as Ronnie completed her math assignment, she was permitted to start on her art work. Thus promptness and correctness in completing her math assignment was an effective way for Ronnie to get rid of an aversive situation. Ronnie was _____ (positively/negatively) reinforced for doing her math work promptly and correctly.

5. One day Ronnie's teacher said to her, "You've been doing so well at your math work that we don't need to do it today. Let's spend an extra hour at art." By doing this, Ronnie's teacher would be combining punishment, negative reinforcement, and _____ to eliminate an undesirable behavior and replace it with a _____ desirable behavior.

6. At the start of the new rules program, Ronnie did her work quickly but carelessly. She found that she could get out of the aversive situation simply by doing her work fast, without caring whether it was correct or not. By letting her start on her art work, Ronnie's teacher was inadvertantly negatively reinforcing an (appropriate/inappropriate) behavior.

7. By changing the contingency--by requiring correct as well as prompt work--Ronnie's teacher made it possible for Ronnie to be negatively reinforced for an (appropriate/inappropriate) behavior.

Answers: 1. Type II.
2. Decrease.
3. None. All it does is decrease the undesirable behavior.
4. Negatively.

51

5. Positive reinforcement.
6. Inappropriate.
7. Appropriate.

Carol: Another Family Example

Carol is three years old. She is playing happily with her five-year-old sister and the four-and six-year-old boys from next door. She wants something with which the younger boy is playing, and he refuses to give it to her. Carol picks up another toy, throws it across the room, and starts to cry. Her father, who has been watching the whole incident, picks Carol up, carries her to her room, sits her down, and says, "You're acting very tired. You'll have to rest here until you can stop crying and feel like you can play with the other kids." Carol stays for fifteen minutes and then rejoins the other children without further incident.

Analysis of Carol:

1. When her father takes Carol to her room after she had thrown a toy and started to cry, this example is of what type of punishment? (Type I, II or III) _____.

2. If this punishment is consistently administered, what behavior(s) is (are) likely to decrease?

3. If this punishment is consistently administered, what behavior(s) is (are) likely to increase?

4. Carol is allowed to come out of her room as soon as she stops crying and feels that she can get along with other children. She is able to eliminate the aversive situation by ceasing her crying and agreeing to cooperate. This action will cause her non-crying and cooperating behaviors to (increase/decrease) because they will be (positively/negatively) reinforced.

5. Instead of waiting until Carol stopped crying and was ready to play, her father could have sent her to her room for fifteen minutes. In this case, for what would Carol be negatively reinforced?

_____
_____
_____
_____

Answers: 1. Type II.

2. Carol's throwing of toys and crying.

3. None. Punishment will merely cause the throwing of toys and crying to decrease. Unless some other specific behavior is <u>reinforced</u>, Carol is perfectly likely to perform some other inappropriate behavior.

4. Increase; negatively. Note that one of the behaviors for which Carol is being reinforced is "non-crying." The reader might legitimately argue that if negative reinforcement causes a behavior to increase, Carol should be taught <u>to do</u> something. Here, all she is being taught <u>to do</u> is to "not cry." This could be construed as semantic double-talk, and will not be discussed in detail here. Perhaps examining how the negative reinforcement could have been appropriately applied will be useful.

5. We don't know. But one possibility would be that Carol would stop crying after five minutes. She would then spend the next ten minutes pouting and plotting how to get even with the other children. If this punishment happened often enough, Carol would actually be reinforced for such pouting and plotting. In other words, by stating the conditions as he did, Carol's father at least took steps to make sure that he would not accidentally be reinforcing an inappropriate behavior. This situation is probably one in which punishment and negative reinforcement should be combined with positive reinforcement. For example, "You sure do play like a big girl," or "You and your friends have been playing so well lately that I'm going to take you and two of your friends to the zoo Saturday."

Paul: An Example from Infancy

Paul was three months old and was usually breast fed. When his mother was not home, he was given a bottle. This feeding method worked quite well, except about one out of five times he would cry uncontrollably and refuse to drink. He obviously was hungry on such occasions, but either because he was <u>too</u> hungry or because he was upset about something else, he could not control himself enough to get hold of the bottle nipple. One day his father was feeding him and in desperation he simply squeezed the baby's mouth and gently shoved it around the nipple. Paul immediately became quiet and consumed the whole bottle. This same procedure worked nearly every time after that when a similar problem arose.

Analysis of Paul:

1. Squeezing and shoving the baby's mouth is an example of (Type I, II or III) punishment.

2. What behavior is likely to decrease as a result of this punishment?

_____

_____

_____

_____

3. The aversiveness stops as soon as the baby starts sucking on the nipple properly. The baby is (positively/negatively) reinforced for sucking properly.

4. As soon as he starts sucking, Paul also starts to receive milk, which he wants very badly. Therefore, Paul is also (positively/negatively) reinforced.

5. The reason this technique worked so effectively for the father was probably because the positive and negative reinforcement occurred simultaneously and (immediately/delayed).

Answers: 1. Type 1.

          2. Probably none. The aversive situation probably bothers Paul, but a baby's response to such aversiveness is to cry--which is one of the behaviors the father wants to elimate. Nevertheless, the baby does notice the aversiveness, and so he also is likely to notice its removal. Therefore an opportunity for negative reinforcement still exists.

          3. Negatively.

          4. Positively.

         5. Immediately. This technique for getting Paul to eat is an effective use of positive and negative reinforcement simultaneously. A similar

phenomenon occurs quite frequently when a baby is born. The mother suffers through a situation which constantly grows more and more aversive. At the height of the aversiveness, the baby is born. The birth of the baby signals the end of the aversiveness (negative reinforcement) and the presence of a new son or daughter (positive reinforcement). This is one reason why "natural" childbirth has been such a satisfying experience for those who have experienced it.

ACCIDENTAL NEGATIVE REINFORCEMENT

One of the outstanding characteristics of negative reinforcement is that it is so often administered <u>accidentally</u>. Consider these common illustrative cases.

<u>Donald: Illustrative Case</u>

Donald is a thirteen-year-old mentally retarded boy. He has always been considered a "good kid," but lately he has been running around with a bad crowd at school and has been getting into trouble regularly. The problem seems to be that the children he used to play with have grown up mentally faster than he has and have started to make fun of him for his shortcomings. The new crowd he runs around with doesn't make fun of him.

Analysis of Donald:

1. For what is Donald being punished?

   _____

   _____

2. The type of punishment is (Type I, II, III).

3. For what behavior is Donald being negatively reinforced?

   _____

   _____

<u>Carmen: Illustrative Case</u>

Carmen is a sixteen-year-old girl. She has always told her mother whatever was on her mind. One day she asked her mother what a four-letter word meant. She received a hour-long lecture on how to be a good girl.

The counselor at school responded the same way. Carmen now discusses sex with her girlfriends instead of her mother or counselor.

Analysis of Carmen:

4. For what behavior is Carmen being punished?

_____

_____

5. For what behavior is Carmen being negatively reinforced?

_____

_____

Bob: Illustrative Case

Whenever Bob's wife finds him around the house drinking beer, she yells at him. Bob now spends a great deal of time at the local tavern.

Analysis of Bob:

6. For what behavior is Bob being punished?

_____

_____

7. For what behavior is Bob being negatively reinforced?

_____

_____

Answers: 1. For associating with his normal friends.

2. Type I.

3. For associating with the "undesirable" friends.

4. For discussing sex with her mother and/or counselor (Type I punishment).

5. For talking about sex with her girlfriends. She probably finds this positively reinforcing, too.

6. For drinking beer in the house.

7. For drinking beer at the tavern.

Let's analyze one such example more specifically.

Mrs. Johnson: An Example

Mrs. Johnson is going through the checkout line at the grocery store. Her daughter Barbie sees the candy and starts to yell and scream, "I want some candy." Since Barbie is making quite a scene, Mrs. Johnson buys her candy.

Analysis of Mrs. Johnson:

Two variables are at work here:

1. Barbie is being <u>positively</u> reinforced (with the candy) for yelling and screaming.

2. Mrs. Johnson is being negatively reinforced (when the yelling and screaming--the embarrassment of annoyance stops) for buying the candy.

The most likely results are that Barbie will continue to yell and scream, and Mrs. Johnson will continue to buy candy. Of course, if Barbie works at it hard enough, Mrs. Johnson eventually may buy the candy even before Barbie starts to yell and scream--an indication of the effectiveness of Barbie's program of negative reinforcement.

Mr. Robinson: A "Time-Out" Example in School

Mr. Robinson is a sixth grade teacher. Robert has been causing a disturbance by grabbing other children's pencils and throwing them in the wastebasket. Mr. Robinson approaches Robert and says, "I'm sorry, Robert, but you'll have to go to the time-out area. Two minutes later Robert shouts to Mr. Robinson, "Hey, can I get out now?" Mr. Robinson replies, "Not yet. Now sit down and act like a gentleman." Robert hollers the same question twelve times in the next ten minutes. Finally, Mr. Robinson relents and lets Robert out of the time-out area.

Analysis of Mr. Robinson:

1. For what behavior is Robert being punished?

   _____

   _____

2. For what behavior is Robert being negatively reinforced?

   _____

   _____

3. Another way to administer the aversive situation would have been to say, "You'll have to go to the time-out room for fifteen minutes." Would this plan have worked better?

   _____

   _____

   _____

Answers: 1. For grabbing pencils and throwing them in the wastebasket.

2. For constantly saying "Hey, can I get out now?"

3. This technique would have at least eliminated Roberts's being negatively reinforced for the undesirable behavior of bothering the teacher. However, no desirable behavior would be reinforced. A better approach might have been to require Robert to stay in the time-out area until he had sat quietly for ten consecutive minutes. This way he would effectively end the aversive situation himself contingent upon his performance of a desired behavior, even though the desirable behavior he performed would be somewhat unrelated to the desirable cooperative behaviors the teacher really wants to teach.

OCCASIONS FOR NEGATIVE REINFORCEMENT

In the examples discussed so far, negative reinforcement can be viewed as the "second half" of punishment. This concept is a useful one: whenever you use punishment, you usually have available to you an opportunity for negative reinforcement. If you fail to use negative reinforcement, you often are missing a good opportunity to teach a person what to do as well as what not to do. This view of negative reinforcement being automatically available whenever punishment is used needs two qualifications:

1. <u>Negative reinforcement can occur in the absence of punishment</u>. The basic prerequisite for negative reinforcement is an aversive situation, and such situations can exist without being preceded by punishment. A person who is bothered by cold breezes will be negatively reinforced for remembering to close the window at night. A student who finds it troublesome to write out English compositions by hand will be negatively reinforced for learning how to type. In these and similar cases it would be unnecessary to maintain that punishment preceded the negative reinforcement. The behaviors are merely reinforced by the removal of aversive conditions which just happen to exist.

2. <u>It is not always feasible to follow punishment with negative reinforcement</u>. For example, a child might be sent to a time-out area because of social misbehavior. Since the child has been removed from social contacts, it is impossible for him or her to be demonstrating desirable social interactions when the punishment is terminated. The closest a parent or teacher might be able to come would be to

obtain from the child a verbal indication that the child intends to interact appropriately. The termination of punishment immediately after this statement of intention would serve to negatively reinforce such statements; and to the extent that such intentions are related to subsequent behaviors, one could say that the desirable behavior is being reinforced. If this reinforcement works (and it probably would work in many cases), use it. But possibly such a procedure would reinforce the child for making promises that he or she has no intention of keeping, and it's obviously a bad idea to reinforce such behavior. If this situation is the case, there is probably no good way that negative reinforcement can be applied to the behavior in question. Even in this case, however, it would be important that the teacher should not terminate the punishment at an inopportune time and accidentally reinforce an undesirable behavior, such as nagging the teacher or making threats to the other students.

Analyzing an aversive situation has two effects. First, when an aversive situation is presented, the situation has the effect of reducing the strength of the behavior which the aversiveness immediately follows. And second, when a aversive situation is removed, it has the effect of increasing whatever caused the behavior's removal. Perhaps the reason why so many punishments fail is because we fail to take advantage of the whole aversive situation.

SUMMARY

An aversive situation has two effects. The onset of an aversive (unpleasant) situation teaches what not to do. The removal of the aversive situation however, has the effect of teaching what to do. This Chapter has focused on negative reinforcement, the removal of aversiveness. By ignoring this very important concept, many parents and teachers either miss a chance to develop positive behaviors after they punish or (even worse) actually reinforce undesirable behaviors without realizing it. Theoretically, a chance is present for negative reinforcement any time a child is punished. However, some kinds of punishment are more easily combined with negative reinforcement of desirable behaviors at their termination than are others. A recommendation is that such techniques be employed whenever possible and that parents and teachers make deliberate use of negative reinforcement in situations when they have already decided that punishment is necessary.

Chapter 4

ALTERNATIVES TO PUNISHMENT

* *

CONTENTS: Positive Reinforcement of Incompatible Behaviors

Extinction

Satiation

Discrimination Training

Differential Reinforcement of Other Behaviors (DRO)

Differential Reinforcement of Low Rates of Response (DRL)

Stimulus Change

Counterconditioning

Summary

* *

Objectives of Chapter 4

After reading this Chapter, you should be able to

(1) define and give examples of each of the techniques in the outline.

(2) identify the advantages and disadvantages of each of these techniques compared to punishment.

Because of the prevalence of negative side effects with punishment, alternative techniques for eliminating undesirable behaviors are often preferred. In the Chapter, two of these alternative techniques will be discussed in detail and six others will be discussed more briefly.

POSITIVE REINFORCEMENT OF INCOMPATIBLE BEHAVIORS

One of the most popular and effective alternatives to punishment is that of positive reinforcement of incompatible behaviors. Positive reinforcement and the related topics of contingency contracting, shaping, fading, and schedules of reinforcement, are the focus of several excellent books on behavior modification. The treatment in this Chapter assumes some knowledge of positive reinforcement, and the more you know about positive reinforcement the better you will be able to apply the technique discussed in this section of Chapter 4. A brief discussion of positive reinforcement was presented in Chapter 2. For more complete treatment, refer to one of the books listed in the Bibliography. The discussion here will focus on how to use positive reinforcement in order to eliminate an undesirable behavior, whereas in other books the focus is on how to increase a behavior.

Positive reinforcement refers to the contingent delivery of a pleasant stimulus. This reinforcement causes the behavior connected with the pleasant behavior to increase. Logically, if one behavior increases, then behaviors which are incompatible with the increased behavior must decrease. Thus, this technique is an indirect attack on the undesirable behavior: the undesirable behavior is eliminated by encouraging its opposite. However, while the undesirable behavior is attacked only indirectly, the outstanding advantage of positive reinforcement is that it directly teaches what to do, instead of merely teaching what not to do.

Reinforcing Desirable Opposite Behaviors

If one examines the behavior problems with which parents and teachers deal, it soon becomes obvious that a very large number of "undesirable" behaviors are really labels applied to the absence of desirable behaviors. Therefore, with such "undesirable behaviors" the most direct approach to their elimination is not punishment, but rather the positive reinforcement of the desired behaviors. Once the child starts to perform the desired behaviors, the "undesirable behaviors" automatically disappear.

Barbara: A Family Example

Barbara is constantly late getting home for supper. Her parents could punish her for her tardiness; and if punishment is effective, she will stop being late. On the other hand, her parents could take the opposite course of action and <u>reward</u> her for getting home on time. If the reward is effective, Barbara will develop the habit of arriving on time for supper; and since being on time is the opposite of being late, Barbara's problem of lateness thus could be eliminated without punishment. (Whether or not Barbara's parents would actually want to choose this second course of action would depend on several factors which will be discussed in this Chapter.)

A large number of "misbehaviors" are similar to Barbara's tardiness in that these misbehaviors are simply the absence of a desirable behavior. The following Reader Response deals with several such examples.

Reader Response--Desirable Opposite Behaviors

Listed below are several undesirable behaviors. All of them are, in reality, the absence of a desirable behavior. Write the desirable opposite behavior in the space provided.

1. Nancy leaves her room a complete mess when she goes out to play.

    Desirable opposite behavior:_____

2. Darin throws his coat on the living room floor whenever he comes into the house.

    Desirable opposite behavior:_____

3. Otis often goes out to play without telling his mother where he is going.

   Desirable opposite behavior:_____

4. Carol starts to work her math problems without reading the directions.

   Desirable opposite behavior:_____

5. Andy pouts and refuses to share his toys with his little brother.

   Desirable opposite behavior:_____

Possible Answers: 1. Nancy cleans up her room before going out.

2. Darin hangs up his coat in the hall closet.

3. Otis tells his mother where he is going.

4. Carol reads her directions before starting her math.

5. Andy shares his toys with his little brother.

While all the problems in the Reader Response could be attacked by punishing the undesirable behavior, these problems can just as easily be attacked by reinforcing the desirable opposite behavior. In fact, in all five cases the desirable opposite appears to be the behavior the parent/teacher really wants to see. If the desired opposite is what the parent/teacher really wants, then reinforcing the desirable behavior would be better than punishing the undesirable behavior. In statement 4 of the Reader Response, effective punishment will stop Carol from starting her math assignment without first reading the directions, but she may start looking for ways to avoid the math assignment altogether! In statement 2, punishment may stop Darin from throwing his coat on the living room floor, but he may instead start throwing it on the basement floor or on the closet floor. The most effective way to develop a desirable behavior is to reinforce that behavior--not punish its absence.

Reinforcing Non-opposite Alternative Behaviors

In the examples discussed so far, a desirable behavior has been the logical _opposite_ of the undesired behavior. Even when such a logical _opposite_ does not exist, positive reinforcement can still be used to eliminate an undesired behavior. As an example, children get into trouble many times because they "have nothing to do." If this statement is accurate, reinforcing <u>any</u> positive or neutral behavior would be a desirable tactic. The theory is that a person can be doing only one thing at a time; and if the person is receiving positive reinforcement for an activity which is at least harmless, then the person will not need to look for destructive ways to obtain reinforcement.

<u>Reader Response: Desirable Non-Opposite Alternative Behaviors</u>:

Listed below are several undesirable behaviors which often occur because a person has not been reinforced for a more desirable behavior. Write two alternative behaviors in the space provided.

1. Mike is a high school senior who throws spitwads during study halls.

    Desirable alternative behavior:_____

    _____

    Desirable alternative behavior:_____

    _____

2. Don grabs toys from his little brother and laughs when the two-year-old cannot get the toys back.

    Desirable alternative behavior:_____

    _____

    Desirable alternative behavior:_____

    _____

Possible Answers: 1. Assuming that Mike enjoys them, any activity similar to the following would be possible:
(a) Let Mike correct papers during study hall.
(b) Give Mike a good book to read.
(c) Let Mike design tests during study hall.

2. (a) Let Don have fun by playing in another room.

(b) Have Don play at the table while his brother plays on the floor.
(c) Pay Don to babysit for his little brother.

Note that by reinforcing a non-opposite alternative behavior, we do not solve the problem; we merely distract the person from the undesirable behavior. The behaviors are incompatible because it's impossible to perform both simultaneously, not because of a logical contradiction. This type of action is purely a temporary measure, and in many cases a temporary measure is all that is needed. However, the child is neither learning what not to do, nor is the child learning a behavior which is contradictory to the undesired behavior. And so, if we wish to increase the chances that the child will make a permanent alteration in behavior, we would have to undertake further procedures.

Combination of Punishment with Positive Reinforcement

What has perhaps already occurred to you is that punishment and positive reinforcement often can be combined. This combination of punishment and positive reinforcement is actually an extremely effective technique: the child not only learns what not to do, but also learns simultaneously what to do. In addition, both the reward and the punishment are intensified by a contrast effect which occurs when the reward and punishment are presented in close association with each other. The following list shows how punishment and positive reinforcement of incompatible behaviors could be combined.

1. Nancy (presented on page 64) could be required to stay in the house when the room is messy (punishment) but could be praised (reward) and permitted to stay out longer (reward) if her room is clean.

2. Mother (page 64) could express disapproval (punishment) to Darin when he throws his coat on the floor and thank him for hanging it in the closet (reward).

3. Otis (page 65) could be allowed to have a party at his house on Friday night (reward) if he tells his mother where he's going each time that week, but he would lose that privilege if he neglected to do so once (punishment).

4. Carol's directions (page 65) could be written in such a way that she'll be able to finish and do something she enjoys (reward) within five minutes if she reads them; whereas if she neglects to read the directions, the assignment will take about half an hour and use up her potential free time (punishment).

5. Andy (page 65) could be praised (reward) when he shares his toys, whereas the toys could be taken away (punishment) for refusing to share.

6. Mike (page 66) could be kept until all the other students have left for lunch (punishment) if he throws spitwads, or he can read a paperback book available in the study hall (reward) if he behaves.

"Darin? You know you're not supposed to throw your coat on the floor?"

7. Don could be sent to his room (punishment) for grabbing his little brother's toys, whereas Mommy and Daddy might join in and play with the two children (reward) if the two seem to be getting along well.

Note that the same rules discussed in Chapter 2 with regard to the negative side effects of punishment still apply in the seven examples just given. With the possibility of such negative side effects in mind, the strategy is often better to use positive reinforcement alone if such undesirable side effects are likely to appear and if the reinforcers are strong. Note also that the combination of punishment and positive reinforcement is especially likely to be effective when Type III punishment (which blends well with positive reinforcement) is employed, as in the case of Otis being allowed to have a party if he tells his mother where he is going all week.

Accidental Behavior Reduction Through Positive Reinforcement

Like punishment, the positive reinforcement of incompatible behaviors can <u>accidentally reduce</u> behaviors which one

really would like to increase. If a parent/teacher wants to increase one behavior but already is strongly reinforcing a behavior which is incompatible with it, then this new behavior will not be taught. Likewise, if a student has been performing a desirable behavior and learns a new behavior which is found to be more reinforcing, that student is likely to decrease the previously learned behavior if the two are incompatible.

Bobby: A Family Example

Bobby has always done chores around the house promptly. One day his mother shows him how to work a certain kind of mathematical puzzle. Bobby does so well that his mother brings him five more puzzles the next day. Bobby again does quite well, and for Christmas he gets several books containing the same kinds of puzzles. Bobby no longer is enthusiastic about his chores. He tries to avoid them and has even stopped doing some of his chores altogether. Puzzles have become a way of life with Bobby.

Caroline: A School Example

Caroline is a fourth grader who always has tried very hard to work her problems in arithmetic. When she gets stuck, she asks the teacher for help. This year the student teacher is a very enthusiastic young man. He comes to Caroline at the beginning of arithmetic period and asks her if she needs help. If she says "No," he goes to help someone else. If she says she needs help, he stays and helps her. Since Caroline likes the attention, she starts asking for more and more help. She no longer tries the problems alone, and even when the student teacher is not present or when he is working with someone else, she still waits for help before she gets started.

Darlene: Another School Example

Darlene does all her assignments in English class. Her teacher thinks she would enjoy Gone with the Wind and loans her a copy of the book. Darlene spends the next three weeks reading the book and does all her assignments quite carelessly during this time.

Reading Gone with the Wind is probably a desirable activity; working math puzzles is at least a neutral, or perhaps even highly desirable activity; and seeking unnecessary assistance is probably an undesirable activity. The important point, however, is that all three of these children have found an activity which is, for them, positively reinforcing and which is incompatible with the behavior the parent/teacher wants to see. Interestingly, if Bobby or Darlene were misbehaving, working puzzles or reading novels would be good activities to reinforce in order to reduce their undesirable behaviors; but in these examples they are reducing desirable behaviors instead. Likewise, seeking help from the student teacher would have been a desirable incompatible behavior which would have reduced copying from another student--if that would have been Caroline's problem--but in her case it is reducing a desirable behavior instead.

The recommendation is not that we try to prevent children from working puzzles or reading novels or stop attending to children's expressed needs, but rather that we become aware of what is being reinforced in a given situation and determine whether or not this behavior is what we really want to reinforce.

Advantages and Disadvantages of Positive Reinforcement of Incompatible Behaviors

The primary _advantages_ of positive reinforcement of incompatible behaviors are these:

1. Positive reinforcement is a positive technique which teaches a person what _to_ do, whereas many of the other techniques discussed in this book merely teach what _not_ to do.

2. Positive reinforcement is unlikely to be accompanied by the negative side effects which were described as accompanying punishment in Chapter 2.

The primary disadvantages of this technique can be summarized as follows:

1. This method is a relatively _indirect_ one for teaching what _not_ to do, and therefore it _is likely_ to be time-consuming and/or ineffective in reaching this goal.

2. The undesired behavior is equivalently subjected to extinction (discussed next in this Chapter), and the shortcomings that apply to extinction apply here.

3. The rewards inherent in the performance of the undesirable behavior may outweigh the rewards offered for the incompatible behavior.

4. The child may tire of the incompatible behavior and revert to the former undesirable behavior.

5. The behavior which you _think_ is incompatible may not actually be incompatible.

These advantages and disadvantages can be summarized by saying that, in general, this positive reinforcement technique is less likely to be accompanied by undesirable side effects; but it is also less likely to work at all. Where efficiency is important, therefore, this technique will best be combined with punishment.

RAPID REVIEW

1. Positive reinforcement is the contingent presentation of a pleasant stimulus. This reinforcement causes a behavior to (increase/decrease).

2. The effect of positive reinforcement is the same as that of
   a. punishment
   b. negative reinforcement
   c. both
   d. neither

3. By reinforcing (strengthening) one behavior one causes a behavior which is incompatible with that behavior to (increase/decrease).

4. Ben never does his homework. Neglect of his homework appears to occur because Ben always forgets to take his books home. Mrs. Martin decides to give Ben one token every time he lines up to go home with his books in his hands. He can later turn in the tokens for any of a large number of rewards. If this system works, what behavior will increase?

   _____

   _____

5. What behavior is likely to decrease for Ben?

   _____

   _____

6. Carla, a fifth grader, likes to climb trees during recess. Carla's tree climbing behavior is dangerous since she climbs quite high and the branches are not very strong. Mrs. Martin puts her in charge of refereeing the third graders' dodge-ball games during recess. A referee is a prestigious position, and Carla really enjoys it.

Which of Carla's behavior is likely to <u>decrease</u>?

_____

_____

7. Mr. and Mrs. Billingham have two sons, 9 and 16, and one daughter, 13 years old. What bothers the parents is that the children are so rude to each other. Often their rude remarks are punctuated with profanity. Since the parents know the children would really like to spend a weekend at Uncle George's cottage in Michigan, they make a deal with the children. The parents will observe the children at times only they themselves will know. If one of the children is doing something nice for one of the others, the children will receive one point. In addition, the parents will make an overall rating on the children each day and give each of the from 5 to -5 points for "politeness performance." If at any time during the day either parent hears profanity directed at one of the other children, this will result in the loss of five points. As soon as the children accumulate 200 points, the family will spend the next weekend at Uncle George's cottage.

What behaviors are likely to <u>increase</u> (provided the reinforcers work)?

_____

_____

8. What behaviors are likely to decrease?

_____

_____

9. Which of the following techniques are the Billinghams employing?
   a. Positive reinforcement
   b. Negative reinforcement
   c. Punishment

Answers: 1. Increase
2. b
3. Decrease
4. Taking books home (and also performance of homework if such performance is truly dependent solely upon the fact that Ben forgets his books).
5. Failure to do homework.
6. Climbing trees.

7. Politeness.
8. Rudeness, profanity.
9. a and c

Summary of Positive Reinforcement of Incompatible Behaviors

The _perfect_ implementation of the positive reinforcement of desired behaviors which are incompatible with undesirable behaviors would totally eliminate the need for punishment. Although such a utopian goal would appear impossible to attain, such a possibility should provide a basis for concerned thought. A vast number of the crimes committed in our society occur primarily because the perpetrators can find their positive reinforcers nowhere else. Ask a group of children in school why they consistently get into trouble, and you'll find they'll claim they have nothing better to do. Experienced observers of young children know that little children don't get into trouble as long as they have something to do, but these angels turn into depraved monsters and do totally unbelievable things when they get bored. Yet Society depends on punishment as a main control tactic! We would laugh at animal trainers who tried to teach animals to perform only by teaching them what _not_ to do--but that's what punishment is designed to accomplish. Parents, teachers, and other social agents would do well to reexamine their current practices and shift emphasis whenever possible to the positive reinforcement of incompatible behaviors rather than mere punitive means of control.

"We would laugh at animal trainers who tried to teach animals to perform only by teaching them what <u>not</u> to do......"

EXTINCTION

The term "extinction" refers to the systematic withholding of reinforcers which had previously maintained a behavior. Supplying reinforcers causes a behavior to increase; withholding the reinforcers makes the behavior decrease or disappear entirely. Thus the effect of extinction is similar to that of punishment. One advantage that extinction has over punishment is that extinction is not as likely to be accompanied by the negative side effect of punishment as discussed in Chapter 2. The main disadvantage is that extinction works more slowly therefore it is less efficient and the undesired behavior is likely to continue for a longer time before it is eliminated.

Factors Influencing the Rate of Elimination of Behaviors

How rapidly a behavior can be eliminated through extinction depends on several factors:

1. <u>The previous reinforcement history of the child</u>. Both the child's reinforcement history in general and the child's history with regard to the specific behavior are likely to be important, although the second is usually the more important factor. If a child has been on a continuous reinforcement schedule (reinforced every time he or she performed the behavior), this behavior will extinguish much more rapidly than if that child has been reinforced on an intermittant schedule (reinforced only occasionally or on an irregular basis). What appears to be happening is that children on continuous schedules have their reinforcers cut off and say to themselves, "Well, I guess I don't get reinforced for that anymore." On the other hand, when we cut off reinforcers from children who have been on intermittant schedules, they seem to say to themselves, "I'd better keep trying. The reinforcers always have come eventually." The latter children are simply harder to convince that the reinforcers are no longer forthcoming.

<u>Bonnie: An Example of Extinction</u>

Bonnie sits in the front row. To get your attention, she sometimes asks useless questions to which she already knows the answers. Every time she raises her hand to ask one of these questions, you call on her, since she is right in front of you anyway. Archie sits in the back left corner. He does the same thing as Bonnie, but you call on him less often, since you don't see him as easily. You decide to eliminate useless questions by not calling on the students unless they are actively involved in their projects.

Reader's Response:

Whose behavior will extinguish most rapidly, Bonnie's or Archie's?

Bonnie's. She's been on a continuous schedule of reinforcement. Likewise, Ben, who comes to school knowing that if he bothers his <u>mother</u> long enough he gets what he wants, is going to be quite persistent if the <u>teacher</u> puts him on an extinction schedule.

2. <u>The number of reinforced trials</u>. If two children have both been reinforced on a continuous schedule, one three times and the other thirty times, the one who has been reinforced

thirty times will be more resistant to extinction than the one who has been reinforced only three times.

3. <u>The deprivation level of the child</u>. The more deprived a child is of attention or the longer it has been since the child received attention, the longer he or she will keep trying to get attention. Likewise, a hungry child will whine for a cookie longer than one who has just eaten. If the child wants attention and the only way to get it is by emitting the undesirable behavior, the undesirable behavior will continue for a very long time; whereas if the child can get attention from a number of sources or in a number of ways, he or she will perform the undesirable behavior for a shorter period of time and then give up and try a different source or approach.

4. <u>The effort needed to make the response</u>. If much effort is required to make a response that is supposed to get attention and this response fails to get attention, then the person is more likely to give up in the face of extinction than if the required response was an easy one to make.

5. <u>The degree to which the reinforcers can actually be withheld</u>. Sometimes only <u>some</u> of the reinforcers can be withheld, and in such cases the behavior will be maintained by those reinforcers which are still being provided. If these other reinforcers are unimportant to the child, the behavior is likely to be extinguished quickly; whereas if these other reinforcers are even more important than the ones being withheld, extinction may not work at all. A clear example of this principle occurs when a behavior is maintained by both teacher attention and peer attention. If only the teacher withholds attention, the behavior may continue unabated; whereas if the teacher is able to enlist the support of some of the peers, the behavior is more likely to undergo extinction.

6. <u>The availability of procedural combinations</u>. The most common techniques combined with extinction are punishment and reinforcement of alternative behaviors. If a child wants attention badly enough, the child will do whatever is necessary to get it. If some other way is provided to get attention (for example, raising a hand), the child can get the attention by this method and not have to persist in the undesirable approach. Thus giving the reinforcer for one behavior eliminates the need for the child to seek the reinforcer through another behavior. Likewise, if the student finds that the teacher is going to ignore a certain behavior 90% of the time and give <u>aversive</u> attention (punishment) the other 10% of the time for that behavior, the student is likely to try another approach to getting more favorable attention if another approach is available.

Thus extinction and punishment can be applied to the <u>undesirable behavior</u> and positive reinforcement can be applied to a <u>desirable alternative behavior</u>. Remember, however, punishment is likely to be accompanied by negative side effects; and so you may want to use only extinction and positive reinforcement of the alternative behavior and omit punishment.

In summary, extinction is likely to work effectively under these conditions:

1. If the child previously has been reinforced on a continuous schedule for a behavior.

2. If reinforcement occurred only a few times.

3. If he or she is not excessively deprived of the reinforcer.

4. If it is a relatively complicated response to make.

5. If all the reinforcers can be withheld.

6. If extinction can be used in combination with punishment or positive reinforcement of an alternative behavior.

On the other hand extinction is less likely to be effective under these conditions:

1. If the child has been reinforced frequently but intermittently in the past.

2. If he or she is relatively deprived of the reinforcer.

3. If the response is an extremely easy response to make.

4. If some reinforcers will still occur.

5. If extinction must be used without the assistance of any other technique.

<u>Extinction Confused with Other Techniques</u>

Extinction is often confused with other techniques. An example might help to distinguish between extinction and Type II punishment. Suppose Billy walks into a room mumbling some new four-letter words he has just picked up from his friend next door. If his parents choose to ignore him, this ignoring behavior is an example of extinction--the nondelivery of the reinforcer (attention) which he was expecting. On the other hand, his parents could sit him in a corner or send him to his room. Both of these latter actions would be examples of Type II punishment--taking away the privilege of the positive reinforcer, personal freedom.

The following analogy to mathematics might help further to differentiate extinction from other techniques:

<u>Positive reinforcement</u> is like <u>addition</u>.

<u>Punishment</u> is like <u>subtraction</u>. (Type III punishment is like addition followed by subtraction.)

<u>Extinction</u> is like <u>non-addition</u> (or the addition of zero).

RAPID REVIEW

1. Extinction refers to the systematic withholding of reinforcers which previously had maintained a behavior. This process will cause a behavior to <u>(increase/decrease)</u>.

2. The effect of extinction is similar to that of
   a. positive reinforcement
   b. negative reinforcement
   c. punishment

3. Extinction usually works <u>(more slowly/more quickly)</u> than punishment in eliminating undesirable behaviors.

4. Extinction is <u>(more likely/less likely)</u> than punishment to be accompanied by negative side effects.

5. A behavior will be eliminated <u>(more quickly/less quickly)</u> through extinction if it has been reinforced on a continuous schedule than if it has previously been reinforced on an intermittent (irregular) schedule.

6. A behavior will be eliminated most quickly if it has been reinforced <u>(frequently/infrequently)</u> in the past.

7. A behavior will be eliminated <u>(more quickly/less quickly)</u> if the person has been deprived of the reinforcer than if ready access to the reinforcer is available.

Answers: 1. Decrease   2. c   3. More slowly   4. Less likely
           5. More quickly   6. Infrequently   7. Less quickly

<u>Attention as a Reinforcer</u>

Very often, when a child is misbehaving, one hears the comment by parents and teachers, "He's doing that to get attention. So let's not give it to him." Such an attitude is not the wisest approach to the problem. A much better comment would be, "He's doing that to get attention. Let's not give him attention <u>for that</u>." The only difference is in the final two words, but they make a huge difference. The point is, if the child wants attention and needs attention, you have a very effective reinforcer at your disposal. Use this reinforcer! Withholding attention for ineffective behavior is only a part of the strategy: applying attention for a desirable behavior is the most important part. To note that extinction occurs quite often <u>by accident</u> is important to note. If children raise their hands in a class but never get called on to give their answer, they will stop raising their hands in that class.

"Amy's just trying to get attention again so I'll ignore her. Of course, I always ignore her."

(Withholding attention for ineffective behavior is only part of the strategy, applying attention for a desirable behavior is the most important part.)

<u>Deliberate Preparation for Subsequent Extinction</u>

Individuals have a few behaviors which parents and teachers have to permit or actually encourage for a short time, but which they know they shall have to eliminate later through the technique of extinction. In such cases, a good idea would be to reinforce the undesirable behaviors on a continuous schedule while permitting them to occur, so that to eliminate the undesirable behaviors when the time comes to do so will be easier.

Examples of Delibarate Preparation for Subsequent Extinction:

Paul was a newborn baby. Since newborn babies cry for a lot of good reasons, including attention, his parents were never sure whether or not to go in and check him when he cried. They knew that when he got older he would cry just for attention, and they didn't want to spend their whole lives rushing to his bedside. For the first six months or so of his life, they attempted to come to his bedside whenever he cried and give him a great deal of attention. Then, when he was six-and-a-half months old, they put him to bed one night, certain that he was well taken care of, and let him scream when he started to cry. After 15 minutes he stopped and went to sleep. The next night he cried for only 5 minutes before going to sleep. Now he still cries once in a while when he is confused or wants something, but in general he quietly goes to sleep when he's put to bed.

David is four years old. Lately he has started coming home and tattling on his friends. His father feels that he doesn't want his son to grow up to be a tattletale, but at the same time he feels that currently he'd like to know about what is happening to his son, because some rather rough kids are in the neighborhood. His strategy is to pay a great deal of attention to his son whenever he tattles for about a year, and then he will cut off his attention and assume a "so what" attitude towards the tattling.

In the previous examples, Paul's crying behavior would have persisted much longer if his parents would have paid attention to his crying on an intermittent rather than a continuous schedule during the first six months. David's father is likely to eliminate tattling more effectively when David is five than if he currently would ignore his son except when he was really interested.

Some Shortcomings of Extinction and How to Overcome Them

In addition to the factors mentioned previously which influence the effectiveness of extinction, the following problems can occur:

1. **Rewards might inadvertantly be given occasionally.** This inadvertent rewarding of behaviors is a very serious problem. Look at this example:

Karim: An Example of Frustrated Extinction

> Karim is a fourth grader who used to be extremely withdrawn. Ms. Harris decided to allow him to make funny faces, thinking that this might bring him out of his shyness. Whenever he makes funny faces, she laughs at him and gives him attention. The problem is that the rest of the class thinks that Karim's face-making behavior is weird, and so the funny faces don't help Karim make friends with the rest of the class. Since Ms. Harris feels that face-making is now a bad thing, she decises to extinguish it by ignoring Karim whenever he makes a funny face. She does this for three days, while Karim continues to make faces. Then on the fourth day Karim makes an especially good face, and Ms. Harris breaks out laughing. Two days later she breaks up laughing again. Karim continues to make faces even though Ms. Harris has ignored him for a week.

What has happened is that Ms. Harris has inadvertently put Karim on an intermittent schedule of reinforcement. His behavior will now be even more resistant to extinction than it was at the beginning of the process. The moral of the story is: if you can't use extinction completely, don't use extinction at all. If Ms. Harris had to give Karim attention at all, she would have been better off giving him aversive attention (punishment) rather than the kind of attention he wanted.

2. **A slight initial increase may occur in the behavior.** What appears to happen is that the child thinks, "Hey! Where's my reward? I'd better try harder." If a child shouts to get the teacher's attention, the child often will respond to extinction by shouting a little longer and louder at first and then dropping off dramatically upon finding that the desired reinforcement is not forthcoming. In some cases you can afford this slight increase in an undesirable behavior. In other cases (such as throwing knives or chairs) you cannot afford such an increase. Expect an initial increase of the undesirable behavior; and if you can stand it, continue to apply the procedure systematically. If all goes well, the behavior will subside. If you cannot stand the initial increase but attempt extinction anyway, you've done more harm than good since the undesirable behavior has been raised to a higher level than if you would have just left the behavior untouched.

3. **Some parents and teachers cannot ignore behaviors effectively.** If this shortcoming applies to you, you're either

going to have to give up a very useful technique or train yourself to ignore some undesirable behaviors. The training would be worth the effort to retain such a valuable behavior control technique.

4. <u>Some behaviors are self-reinforcing</u>. Ignoring a child for cheating on a test would not reduce cheating behavior-- except in the very rare cases when children actually do this cheating because of a need to get attention. The reward for cheating is getting the right answers and doing well on the test. <u>Those</u> rewards would have to be removed for extinction to be effective.

5. <u>Intense misbehaviors cannot be ignored</u>. What is good for the individual must be at least harmless to others. If much harm is likely to occur by letting a behavior continue, some form of punishment might be the more appropriate procedure.

"<u>Some</u> intense misbehaviors cannot be ignored!"

6. <u>Old habits sometimes recur.</u> The child may try an old trick to see if the trick will work again under new circumstances, even though this behavior had been extinguished previously. If such a recurrance of behavior happens, simply reextinguish the behavior. If this recurrence happens too often, then combining punishment with the extinction procedure might make the behavior less likely to appear again.

7. <u>New misbehaviors might appear.</u> This new misbehavior is likely to happen when extinction is used alone, because--like punishment--this new misbehavior teaches what <u>not</u> to do, not what <u>to</u> do. If new misbehaviors occur, you can always submit them also to an extinction procedure. This whole problem can be avoided by building positive reinforcement for an alternative behavior into your extinction program.

<u>Extinction vs. Punishment</u>

Often argued is the idea that extinction is a more humane technique and should therefore be given precedence over punishment as a behavior-management technique. That extinction is a more humane technique is not necessarily the case. To take an extreme example, autistic children* can have these self-stimulatory behaviors reduced or eliminated through extinction, but this technique is indeed a slow process. Igar Lovaas has found that by giving such children a very slight number (often only 2 or 3) of harmless electrical shocks while they're engaging in self-destructive behavior, this self-stimulation stops almost immediately! These autistic children, who were previously impervious to their environments, can then start to accept positive reinforcers and begin to live a happier life. Very few people actually would charge that such punishment is more inhumane than the alternative of strapping autistic children into beds for the rest of their lives or letting them pound their heads on the wall until they get tired of such behavior. (One study recorded that an autistic child banged his head on the wall 25,000 times before stopping.)

The same logic can be applied to non-autistic children. Are we really being more humane to let a child be rude to other children for two months if we could stop such behavior in one day through punishment? This line of reasoning can, of course, be abused. I am certainly not recommending that punishment be immediately invoked in every case, and I hope that's not the impression given in this book. What I am suggesting is that

---

*Autistic children often engage in several self-destructive and self-stimulatory behaviors to such an extent that they cannot interact with their environment.

when we decide whether to use extinction or punishment, the appropriate procedure would be to weigh the advantages of punishment, (it's efficient) and its disadvantages (it has negative side effects) against the advantages of extinction (relative freedom from side effects) and its disadvantages (relatively inefficient). The question is which of these behavior modifiers is the appropriate technique to use in an individual situation, not which is a priori a more humane strategy.

Summary of Extinction

A final word. Extinction does work. It works when a specific undesired behavior is being performed to obtain a specific reward, such as attention. When these "specifics" are the case, you will often be astonished to find that by removing the reinforcer for the undesirable behavior and supplying it instead for a desirable behavior, extinction works remarkably quickly. Thus under these circumstances, the combination of extinction and positive reinforcement of a desirable behavior accomplishes the goal as efficiently as punishment and with no negative side effects. In such cases extinction is clearly the preferred strategy.

SATIATION

The term satiation refers to the technique of simply letting the reinforcers occur for the behavior until they cease to be reinforcing. Once the reinforcers lose their value, then the behavior is likely to "self-reduce." People stop eating when they have had enough, even though eating originally was quite reinforcing. An avid fishing enthusiast likewise reaches a point where, at least temporarily, fishing loses its reinforcing value.

Hank: A School Example

The teacher sees Hank throwing a wad of paper across the room toward the wastebasket. She wants him to stop this act. She tells him to move a little closer and hands him a stack of scrap paper and tells him to throw until he feels he's tired of it. The next day she lets him do the same thing. He tires much more quickly. The third day he doesn't even bother.

Hank has simply grown tired of throwing paper wads. Since throwing paper wads is no longer reinforcing, he stops. Note that this principle is different from that of the technique of "negative practice" discussed in the next Chapter. The use of negative practice would require Hank to throw paper wads into the wastebasket for a couple of hours--until he hated the sight of paper wads.

Shortcomings of Satiation

    A major shortcoming of satiation is that the effects often are only temporary. A week or so later Hank, our school example, may decide to throw paper wads again. With satiation, the parent or teacher is merely given a reprieve, during which time the student can learn a more adaptive behavior. Another shortcoming is that some behaviors take a long time to hit the satiation point, and in such cases an alternate technique may be in order. A final problem with satiation is that this technique can be applied only to behaviors which the teacher/parent can put up with for as long as it takes for satiation to occur. If a behavior is especially bothersome to the parent or teacher, a more efficient technique would be appropriate.

DISCRIMINATION TRAINING

Some behaviors are appropriate in certain situations, but not in others. For example, for Joey to joke about a mental mistake his big brother makes is appropriate, but it might be entirely inappropriate to joke about the same type of mistake if it were made by the mentally retarded boy next door. Such situations call for discrimination training: the child needs to learn how to discriminate when a response is appropriate from when it is not.

The procedure for teaching such discriminations is actually quite simple: regularly reinforce the specified behavior in the presence of the appropriate stimuli, and place that same behavior on an extinction or punishment schedule in the presence of the inappropriate stimuli. The parent or teacher must help the child to identify the important characteristics of the appropriate and inappropriate situations and then apply the proper differential reinforcement.

Becky: A School Example

Becky laughs loudly whenever something funny happens on the playground. But she laughs equally loudly in the classroom, and this is extremely distracting to the rest of the class. The teacher talks to Becky privately and points out to her when it is a good idea to laugh loudly and when this is a bad idea. The next day, when Becky laughs loudly in the classroom, the teacher looks at her sternly and says "Not now!" Later, out on the playground, Becky laughs loudly several times, and each time the teacher goes over and joins in the laughter with her.

Analysis:

Becky is being punished (Not now!" for laughing in the inappropriate situation (classroom), but is being reinforced (teacher attention) in the appropriate situation (playground). Two alterations might have been necessary to improve this procedure:

1. Resorting to a different reward or punishment if either proved ineffective.

2. Clarifying the stimulus situations further if Becky could not easily make the discrimination.

A further discrimination that the teacher probably will want to teach Becky is that it's still OK to laugh quietly, but not loudly, in the classroom. This discrimination could be taught by laughing with Becky when she laughs quietly and by sternly saying "No!" or "Quietly" when she laughs too loudly. A good idea is to teach one discrimination at a time.

Discrimination Training as an Aid to Overcoming Negative Side Effects of Punishment

Note that this process of discrimination training has previously been mentioned in Chapter 2 in the discussion of the negative side effects of punishment. When punishment is administered, it often eliminates more behaviors than need to be eliminated; and discrimination training can help to prevent such overgeneralization.

DIFFERENTIAL REINFORCEMENT OF OTHER BEHAVIOR (DRO)

Differential reinforcement of other behavior is a rather extreme technique. The parent or teacher reinforces every behavior _except_ one specific target behavior on a regular basis. This technique is a very powerful one, since the child usually has several desirable behaviors available to perform and will usually be willing to select one of these instead of the target behavior. However, quite possibly some of these alternative behaviors also are undesirable. If some behavior needs to be eliminated rapidly and at all costs, the DRO might be a good technique, especially if other techniques have proven ineffective or appear to be impractical.

Henrietta: An Example of DRO

> Henrietta picks her nose a lot. Her parents tell her that she will get a point every thirty seconds if she is doing anything other than picking her nose. Henrietta quickly earns 100 points and is allowed to go to a movie.

Note that DRO is a temporary technique. What the technique accomplishes for Henrietta is that it gets her temporarily to stop a behavior which previously had been automatic. Other techniques would be needed to make the change permanent. A problem which frequently seems to accompany this technique is the restriction of the change to the training situation. For example, Henrietta might stop picking her nose when her parents are training her but then go off to the theatre and pick her nose while she watches the movie. Another problem is that Henrietta might be reinforced for some other undesirable behaviors while she's not picking her nose. For example, she gets points for sucking her thumb, kicking the dog, and pulling her sister's hair. Therefore, use this technique _only_ when you're desperate or when the child is highly likely to perform only desirable behaviors in place of the target undesirable behavior.

DIFFERENTIAL REINFORCEMENT OF LOW RATES OF BEHAVIOR (DRL)

Sometimes a parent or teacher simply wants to reduce the frequency with which a behavior occurs rather than eliminate it entirely. For example, for Ted to ask his mother to pass the salt when he needs it is appropriate, but such a request is inappropriate if it occurs five times in a minute. The same principle applies to Ted's asking the teacher if he can go out to get a drink of water. In such cases, the parent/teacher could reinforce the behavior when it occurs at appropriately spaced intervals; but put it on an extinction or punishment schedule when the behavior happens too frequently.

Howie: An Example of DRL

Howie constantly asks to be allowed to go out for a drink of water. The teacher has reason to believe that he is not dying of thirst. So she tells Howie that his requests to get a drink of water will be ignored unless at least an hour has elapsed since his last request. Howie arrives at school the next day, and promptly asks to be allowed to get a drink. The teacher says OK and jots down the time. Ten minutes later, Howie asks again. This time the teacher simply jots down the time (9:10) and ignores Howie. At 9:25 Howie asks again, and again the teacher jots down the time and ignores him. At 10:30 Howie asks again. This time he is permitted to get his drink.

You may have noticed that this technique is really a specific type of discrimination training. Howie is being required to make accurate discriminations between appropriate and inappropriate intervals after which to ask permission to get his drink.

STIMULUS CHANGE

Sometimes a behavior occurs only in the presence of certain specific stimuli, but not in the presence of others. In such specified cases, the behavior often can be eliminated simply by removing the child from the one stimulus situation and putting him or her in another.

Examples of Stimulus Change:

Lenny is very talkative when he sits next to Susan. The teacher moved him three seats away from Susan and Lenny is still happy but much quieter.

Bruce's mother comes into the room and says, "Don't any of you kids climb up to the top of the bookcase and break my new lamp." This idea had never occurred to any of the children before. When she returns to the room, the lamp is broken and the children are gone. Bruce's mother probably should have kept quiet about the potential problem in the first place.

Whenever Mrs. Johnson gives her students a five-minute lecture on honesty before a test, somebody cheats. When she just gives them the test without mentioning the subject of honesty, nobody cheats. Mrs. Johnson should stop lecturing.

In the previous examples, the undesirable behaviors occur only in the presence of certain stimuli (Susan's presence, a warning about the lamp, and a lecture on cheating). By removing the stimuli, there is nothing left to trigger the undesirable behaviors.

A Specific Type of Stimulus Change

A specific type of stimulus change advocated by the psychologist Fritz Redl is called "Anticeptic Bouncing." In this approach, when the parent or teacher sees that a problem is going to occur between two children, one of the children is removed from the situation. For example, if Ms. Jones can tell from previous experience that Bobby is going to fight with Johnny in the next few seconds, she can send Bobby to the principal's office on an errand (not as a punishment). While Bobby is gone, she can talk to Johnny. By the time Bobby returns, he also may have cooled down. In this way the whole problem can be prevented by this simple temporary change of stimuli.

Shortcomings of Stimulus Change

A major shortcoming of stimulus change is that stimulus change is only temporary. Children who do not have positive behaviors in their repertoire will soon start performing the undesirable behavior in modified stimulus situations. What this technique does is give the parent/teacher a chance temporarily to remove the undesirable behavior and teach a new behavior in its place. The major advantage of this technique is that it is relatively positive and free from negative side effects.

Stimulus change can involve the addition of a triggering stimulus, as well as the removal of one. For example, if Tim chews gum in the classroom only because he forgets where he is, a simple quiet reminder of "Remember, no gum!" will keep him from chewing gum in the classroom. The Ancient Sage narrates the story of the parents who were troubled because their son neglected to say his prayers before going to sleep at night. Having read this chapter in an ancient scroll, the parents said to the child just as he was climbing into his bed, "Haven't you forgotten something?" The child replied, "Oh yeah!" and promptly ran off to go to the bathroom. Be sure that the stimulus really does evoke the behavior you want it to evoke.

COUNTERCONDITIONING

Another way to eliminate a behavior is to build an emotional state which militates against the undesirable response. This technique is referred to as counterconditioning. When a person wants to do something (such as smoke or consume alcohol) and he or she conditions himself or herself emotionally to oppose this tendency, the process is usually referred to as <u>aversive counterconditioning</u>. When the person is afraid to do something and wants to stop this irrational fear, that person can reverse the counterconditioning process and make himself or herself less emotionally hesitant to perform the activity. This is referred to as <u>desensitization</u>. (Both of these techniques are based on what psychologists refer to as classical conditioning, whereas the other techniques discussed in this book are based on operant conditioning.) A full treatment of this subject would require a detailed discussion of classical conditioning, and therefore only a brief description of these techniques will be given here. They are included only for the sake of completeness.

Suppose Arnie wants to stop smoking. He could do so by conjuring up in his mind some vile picture which almost makes him vomit. Then whenever he reaches for a cigarette, he could bring this picture back into his mind. Since the smoking would be associated with an unpleasant emotional state, Arnie would be less likely to enjoy the cigarette; and through the continued application of this approach he might give up smoking completely. (Either that or he'd start liking the vile picture a little better!) Thus this process of counterconditioning is really a matter of associating a pleasant activity with an unpleasant object or activity, with a resulting disinclination toward the formerly pleasant activity.

<u>Accidental Behavior Elimination as a Side Effect</u>

Like the other procedures discussed in this book, aversive counterconditioning often discourages behaviors <u>by accident</u>. For example, some college students who have had unpleasant experiences with mathematics absolutely refuse to study statistics if this subject is approached from a mathematical point of view; whereas if they are introduced to the subject without being aware that it has a major mathematical basis, they study it quite avidly.

Systematic Desensitization

Suppose, on the other hand, that Arnie is afraid of snakes. We could then have Arnie conjure up in his mind some very pleasant image and then show him pictures at first very remotely relating to snakes and then very closely involving snakes. Next we could take Arnie, while he's still imagining some pleasant things or is at least in a relaxed state, and gradually have him come closer and closer to touching snakes. Eventually Arnie could be taught to let the harmless little boa constrictor crawl around his neck, and this wouldn't scare him a bit! By the process of systematic desensitization we would have eliminated Arnie's previous behavior of being afraid of snakes. Similar procedures using systematic desensitization could be applied to other irrational fears, such as fear of public speaking, fear of school, fear of high places, etc.

SUMMARY

Presented in this Chapter were eight techniques other than punishment for teaching a person not to do something. In general, these techniques vary in the following ways:

1. In the specific kinds of problems to which they can be applied.

2. In the efficiency with which they are likely to operate.

3. In the probability that they will be accompanied by the negative side effects which often accompany punishment.

The advantages, disadvantages, and guidelines for applying these techniques were discussed in this Chapter and are summarized schematically in Table 7.1 of Chapter 7. In Chapter 7 these techniques will be integrated with other techniques in order to help you evaluate specific, concrete situations and make practical decisions about what technique to apply.

Chapter **5**

SPECIAL KINDS
OF
PUNISHMENT

* *

CONTENTS: Systematic Exclusion (Time-Out)

Response Cost

Negative Practice

Overcorrection

Covert Punishment

Vicarious Punishment

Corporal Punishment

Summary

* *

Objectives of Chapter 5

After reading this Chapter, you should be able to

(1) identify examples of each of the techniques discussed in this chapter and

(2) identify the relative advantages and disadvantages of each of these techniques.

The material in Chapter 2 presented the three basic types of punishment. Chapter 5 will apply the principles of Chapter 2 to specific techniques for administering punishment. This Chapter certainly will not cover every possible way to administer an aversive stimulus, but rather will examine several major punishment techniques in terms of the characteristics which make them unique and effective or ineffective.

SYSTEMATIC EXCLUSION (TIME-OUT)

Time-Out is an example of Type II punishment. This technique involves removing the child from a source of reinforcement for a designated period of time. The old-fashioned technique of having a child sit in the corner is often a time-out strategy. The assumption behind time-out is that the child finds the current stimulus setting a pleasant one and would like to continue being there. When removed from that setting therefore the child regards the removal as an aversive turn of events, and hence as an example of Type II punishment. To the extent that the current situation is an unpleasant one or the situation into which the child will be placed is regarded as more pleasant than the current one, then the attempt at time-out would be reinforcement rather than Type II punishment. This principle is the underlying one behind the fact that requiring a disobedient child to sit in the corner doesn't work if the child wants to be left alone anyway. Likewise, sending a child to a room if it is full of toys or to the principal's office where the child can talk to all the visitors who come in will often be positively reinforcing rather than punishing.

Examples of Time-Out:

Charlene constantly fights with her friends. Her mother sees Charlene fighting and tells Charlene to come into the house, commenting: "If you can't play right with your friends, you can't play with them at all." About a half hour later, Charlene is allowed to go back outside, with the warning that if there is any more fighting, she'll have to come in again.

Buba whispers to his friends in class. Mrs. Hernandez sends him to a part of the room where she can keep an eye on him, but where he cannot see or be seen by the rest of the class. She lets him return to his seat after he has worked quietly for fifteen minutes.

Advantages of Time-Out

The relative freedom from negative side effects often makes time-out a good technique to use. Time-out has the additional advantage of being easy to combine with negative reinforcement at its termination. Mr. Robinson's treatment of Robert in Chapter 3 (page 58) is a good example of such a combination. Sending a child out of the room, detention after school, keeping the child in from recess, and suspension from school or from a class <u>can</u> all be effective time-out procedures, provided the child really wants to be engaged in the activity from which he or she is being removed.

Guidelines for Using Time-Out

In addition to the general guidelines for punishment, the following guidelines are useful when implementing time-out procedures:

1. <u>Remove all the reinforcers</u>. If Tommy is allowed to take his favorite book with him, if he can watch the girls' volleyball team practicing, or if the principal tells him jokes, the child is being placed in a <u>reinforcing situation, not a punishing situation.</u> Likewise, if Jane is kept after school and then the teacher talks to her sympathetically about the problems of her home life, while this may sometimes be a good idea, it is not time-out. The time-out environment should be a neutral environment, free from either pleasant or unpleasant stimuli. Putting a child in a dark closet is <u>not</u> time-out. Being placed in a dark closet rather would be Type I punishment--the presentation of an aversive stimulus--and is usually a very bad idea because of the negative side effects. Putting the child in the hall is often ineffective, since he or she gets lots of visitors, which can be positively reinforcing. Putting a child in an empty office or lighted cloak room would be better--unless the child can derive pleasure from going through drawers and coat pockets. I have found that a good technique is to place a portable blackboard in front of the room, blocking the child's view so that I can see the child but the child cannot interact with any of the other children in the room. This way I can remove any reinforcers he or she happens to find.

2. <u>Keep the time-out as short as possible</u>. Since the child is removed from the learning environment while in the time-out area, he or she is missing opportunities to practice desirable behaviors as well as the undesirable one. Missing the opportunity to practice positive behavior could be harmful, so you want to get that child back in action as soon as possible. Therefore, the time-out should be just long

enough to be aversive to the child and short enough not to waste his or her time.

3. <u>Don't give time-out from aversive situations</u>. If you do, you're negatively reinforcing whatever behavior the child performed to get the time out, and you'll <u>increase</u> rather than <u>decrease</u> the undesirable behavior. If a child hates school and can most easily get suspended by smoking, that child is likely to become a chain smoker at a very young age. Actually, exclusion from school rarely is perceived as an aversive situation, especially by students who repeatedly are suspended. The mere fact that a student is not deterred from an activity after his or her first suspension suggests that the student does not regard absence from school as punishing. (On the other hand, suspending an especially disruptive student does remove an aversive stimulus from the classroom, and the other students and the teacher might benefit from this removal, even if it does nothing for the suspended student.)

RESPONSE-COST

Response-cost is another example of Type II punishment. Response-cost differs from time-out in that it involves the removal of a specific <u>amount</u> of reinforcers rather than loss of reinforcement for a period of <u>time</u>. This technique could involve the loss of tokens or the loss of points toward a grade.

Jim--An Example of Response-Cost:

Jim has been working on a token reinforcement system. He gets one token for every ten arithmetic problems he solves correctly. Jim has discovered that if he works quickly but carelessly, he can turn in twenty items, get half of them wrong, and still get a token for the ten correct. His teacher notices this loophole and changes the rules so that Jim gets one token for every correct answer, but loses two tokens for every incorrect answer. Since he realizes he will be penalized for careless work, Jim slows down and performs his work with near-perfect accuracy.

Used consistently and fairly, response-cost is a relatively powerful and convenient strategy for bringing about rapid reduction of behaviors.

Guidelines for Employing Response-Cost

In addition to the general guidelines for administering punishment, the following guidelines will be helpful in employing response-cost.

1. Allow the person to accumulate a sufficient supply of reinforcers. With a token system, if the person can collect several tokens and even trade some of them for a back-up reinforcer, he or she will place a higher value on the tokens and consequently be more concerned about losing them.

2. Penalize sparingly and fairly. If you remove all the tokens or points, you've used your last means of response-cost control. If the child views the whole situation as hopeless, he or she will stop looking for the reinforcers which could have been earned and seek rewards from some other source, perhaps in undesirable behavior.

3. Allow opportunities to regain lost reinforcers. These opportunities combine positive reinforcement for desirable behaviors with punishment for the undesirable behavior. In addition, if you don't provide opportunities to regain lost reinforcers, the child may lose interest in the reinforcement program and seek reinforcers elsewhere. One caution: if you give the reinforcers back too easily, then the punishment loses its effectiveness because the cost becomes almost insignificant.

NEGATIVE PRACTICE

With the technique called negative practice the child is required to repeat a pleasant behavior to the point where it assumes an aversive association. This technique works especially well with uncontrolled, involuntary behaviors which a person would like to eliminate but cannot.

Examples of Negative Practice:

Lydell wanted to quit smoking but couldn't. One day he bought a carton of cigarettes and forced himself to smoke the whole carton in one evening. He hasn't touched a cigarette in nineteen years. His problem now is that he feels sick when other people smoke around him.

Viola bit her fingernails. She wanted to stop but couldn't. One day she bit them until they hurt. The next day when she brought her hand to her mouth, the pain was still there; and so she consciously withdrew her hand. Even after the actual pain was gone, its memory remained. Viola no longer unconsciously bites her fingernails.

Jan was throwing paperwads across the room one day. The teacher asked him to stay after class and handed Jan a stack of 100 sheets of scrap paper and instructed him to wad them up and throw them into the basket. If he missed, he was required to pick that piece up and try again. When Jan finished, the teacher dumped the wastebasket in front of Jan and told him to try it again. Jan did this ten times. He no longer enjoys throwing paperwads.

Some Cautions on Negative Practice

Note that this technique could border on cruelty. A problem similar to Jan's was treated by satiation in Chapter 4.

One prerequisite is that negative practice will be successful _only_ if the behavior is actually repeated to the point where it becomes aversive; otherwise negative practice could actually result in a strengthening of the behavior through practice. A second prerequisite in the case of voluntary treatment (such as Lydell and Viola--the examples just given) is that the person must be strongly motivated to change the behavior. Since negative practice is a rather harsh technique, it is likely to be accompanied by negative side effects except, of course, when it is undertaken voluntarily.

Accidental Negative Practice

Negative practice often can and does occur **by accident**. Parents and teachers sometimes find that a behavior is so rewarding to a child that they insist that the child perform the behavior to such an extreme extent that the behavior not only reaches a satiation point, but that behavior actually becomes aversive to the child. The classic example is the child who likes to play the piano and the parents (often because of a financial investment) insist that the child keep at it. Often such children grow to hate music.

OVERCORRECTION

In overcorrection the child is required to correct an inappropriate behavior to an extreme degree and/or to over-compensate for any undesirable results which occurred because of the behavior. This technique is most easily explained through an example.

Example of Successful Use of Overcorrection:

Joan sucks on her hand inappropriately. She sucks her hand automatically and cannot stop herself. Her mother decides that whenever Joan sucks her hand Joan will be stopped immediately and taken to the bathroom, where she will be required to wash her mouth out with a vile-tasting liquid, have her mouth cleaned with a brush, and have her lips washed very firmly and thoroughly. Such a process takes up a very unpleasant five minutes for Joan. After this process occurs four times, Joan stops the inappropriate mouthing behavior and never repeats it again.

Possible Negative Side Effects of Overcorrection

Overcorrection has been found to be a very powerful technique. It also could be a very harsh technique (accompanied by numerous negative side effects) unless it is administered non-vindictively, as a necessary and automatic result of the inappropriate behavior.

Overcorrection is similar to negative practice in that they both take a previously automatic, involuntary, but pleasant activity and turn it into a conscious and unpleasant activity. Overcorrection is rarely used, partly because of the possibility of negative side effects and partly because of the restricted number of activities to which it is appropriately applied. In most cases some other technique would be better. Problems to which overcorrection can sometimes be applied are thumb-sucking, nosepicking, head-banging, smoking, and similar involuntary behaviors.

COVERT PUNISHMENT

Until recently, theorists and researchers in the field of behavior modification have focused entirely on external, observable behaviors to which to apply their techniques. Currently, it is becoming obvious that thoughts are susceptible to many of the same influences applicable to overt behaviors. Indeed, thoughts are observable events if only to the person who thinks them. The term covert conditioning has been applied to the whole group of techniques which apply the tactics discussed in this book to thought processes.

Covert Punishment as an Internal Process

A person can eliminate a thought by punishing himself or herself whenever this specific thought occurs. The whole process can be internal: the person thinks the undesirable thought, and as soon as the thought occurs, switches to another thought which is aversive, and thus the specific thinking behavior is punished.

Examples of Covert Punishment:

Gerald is a juvenile delinquent who would like to reform but compulsively steals cars. He finds himself daydreaming quite frequently about his planned thefts. His counselor tells him that every time he fantasizes a car theft in the future he should immediately shift his thoughts to something as unpleasant as possible. Thereafter, whenever Gerald realizes he is daydreaming about a car theft, he imagines a huge dog jumping out of the car at him and his girl friend laughing at him for being afraid of the dog. Gerald is being covertly punished for daydreaming about car thefts. Since he knows that Gerald daydreams a lot and will continue to do so, the counselor goes one step further. He recommends that Gerald covertly

<u>reinforce</u> himself by daydreaming about more socially acceptable things.

Julie is an obese adolescent. She finds that she eats when she is not even remotely hungry. She reasons that if she could stop thinking about food, she would stop feeding her face. And so, whenever she thinks about a delicious snack, she immediately thinks about something extremely disgusting (such as vomit) covering the snack. She stops thinking about food and becomes thin.

Eve was afraid to speak to men at parties. To combat this problem, she deliberately thought of herself falling off a high building. As soon as she had this picture vividly in her mind, she suddenly switched to a scene of her calmly talking to a nice man at a party, discussing her hobbies, her work, etc. (This is <u>covert negative reinforcement</u>. The unpleasant thought of falling off a high building is obliterated when Eve vividly pictures the party scene. She is therefore negatively reinforced for thinking her new thought.)

These examples differ from counterconditioning (discussed in Chapter 4) in that in counterconditioning the two thoughts are <u>paired</u>, whereas in covert punishment the aversive thought comes <u>immediately after</u> the undesirable thought.

Covert Punishment as a Partially External Process

The process does not have to be completely internal. Internal thoughts can be modified by altering external conditions.

I have tried this process myself. In playing racquetball, I found myself running around the court and hitting the ball without concentrating on aiming the ball to get it past my opponent. Therefore, I made the following agreement with myself: If I did not first say to myself "Think" and form a specific strategy, I would withdraw the privilege of swinging at the ball. The situation was really quite embarrassing to catch up with the ball, get set, and then not swing; but after this happened a few times, I started concentrating much better. Now I plan almost all my shots and play a much better game.

Additional Use of Covert Techniques

In addition to punishment, covert techniques can be applied to almost all the other tactics discussed in this book, although in fact very little research is reported in this area. Covert reinforcement of incompatible desirable thoughts is an obvious possibility: as soon as the person thinks a specified target thought, he or she either thinks a reinforcing thought or performs a reinforcing activity. In covert negative reinforcement, the person would terminate an aversive thought or behavior contingent upon having thought the desired target thought.

Developments in this area are extremely recent. The leading researcher and theorist at this time is Joseph Cautela, and you may want to refer to his works for further details on this rather intriguing subject.

VICARIOUS PUNISHMENT

When a child watches someone else being punished for a behavior, the effect often is similar to actually punishing the child: the observing child is less likely to perform the behavior. (This effect is similar to reinforcing a model, discussed in Chapter 2.) The punishment administered to the model is most likely to influence the observer's behavior under these conditions:

1. If the model is similar to the observer.

2. If the model has a certain degree of prestige.

3. If the behavior for which the model was punished is easily observable.

An important factor however is that the punishment is indirect as far as the observer is concerned whereas the reinforcers that might be attached to the observer's usual behavior are perceived as direct, and therefore sometimes even a rather severe vicarious punishment is ineffective. This principle explains why people killed the King's deer in medieval England even though the punishment was immediate execution, and why high school students frequently sneak a smoke in the restroom even in the face of dire punishments. The deer and the cigarette are there, whereas the punishments happen to "someone else."

Effectiveness of Vicarious Punishment

Nevertheless, vicarious punishment definitely often does work: children do stop doing things that they see others being punished for. Vicarious punishment creates a sort of "ripple effect." Because of this effect, that vicarious punishment and its accompanying side effects will occur <u>by accident</u> is extremely likely. When one child is punished, that child may know exactly for what he or she is being punished; but several observers may know only that a punishment has occurred for some behavior which they observed. If the observers want to avoid punishment, they will avoid doing what they <u>think</u> the model did to get punished. For example, if the model is punished for cracking ethnic jokes which the teacher views as insulting to one of the other students, the observers might try to avoid punishment by never telling jokes, by keeping much more quiet during class, by not raising their hands any more, or by being less creative--depending on what behavior they perceived to be punished.

Cautions on Vicarious Punishment

The possibility of accidental vicarious punishment occurring does not mean that you should become paranoid about punishing one child for fear of the effects on others. What you should do is become aware of the possibility of such effects and take steps to minimize them when you want them minimized and to maximize them when you really want to teach several children at the same time what not to do.

A word of caution: "Making an example" of a child can intensify the punishment and increase the negative side effects. Vicarious punishment can often be administered, however, without holding the model up to public ridicule.

Note also that negative reinforcement (Chapter 3) can occur vicariously (either intentionally or by accident). An observer will imitate whatever he or she thinks a model did to avoid or escape from a punishing situation.

CORPORAL PUNISHMENT

Largely because of ethical considerations and personal convictions, most people find difficulty in giving the topic of corporal punishment an objective evaluation. The allegation by organizations such as the American Civil Liberties Union that corporal punishment is a form of "cruel and unusual punishment" and hence violates the constitutional rights of children is frequently countered by equally impassioned replies that "Children need discipline" or "My Dad beat me when I acted up, and I'm eternally grateful to him for doing it." A. S. Neill's suggestion in Summerhill that the only reason parents spank children (aside from a little sexual pleasure!) is because they hate the children is quite understandably interpreted as absurd, for many parents know that punishing children really does hurt them more than it hurts the children. The Supreme Court has ruled (April, 1977) that corporal punishment does not automatically violate the constitutional rights of school children.

Amid all the rhetoric, what scientific facts are there? Surprisingly few. Nobody has really demonstrated that corporal punishment has the desired long-lasting effects that such punishment is supposed to have on behavior. On the other hand, nobody has proved that corporal punishment really does any harm. The employment of extreme tactics--either physically abusing children on the one hand or spoiling them on the other--both have extremely negative results; but here again, it's hard to say which technique is worse.

Pros and Cons of Corporal Punishment

The fact that most normal American adults have grown up in families and in schools where corporal punishment was an accepted procedure suggests that the evils supposedly inherent in it probably are exaggerated. By following the guidelines in Chapter 2 of this book with regard to punishment in general --especially by

1. focusing on a specific behavior,

2. telling the child what the behavior is, and

3. then punishing the specific behavior rather than communicating a general hatred or dislike for the child,

many parents have undoubtedly accomplished a great deal of good through the use of corporal punishment.

On the other hand, the arguments that we have to use corporal punishment also fail to stand close scrutiny. Such arguments usually go something like, "You have to spank kids. My next door neighbor never spanks his kids, and they're the worst brats I've ever seen!" This argument would make sense if the only alternative to spanking were to do absolutely nothing about misbehaviors. In reality, however, many other forms of punishment might, if given the chance, turn out to be much more effective than spanking.

The one clear advantage of corporal punishment is that it often can be delivered immediately and be over with quickly. Children often perceive this advantage of corporal punishment; and many children will make remarks such as, "Couldn't you just spank me and get it over with and then let me go to the movies?" However, this advantage shrinks considerably if the child has to wait till the father gets home to receive the spanking or if someone other than the teacher has to be summoned in order to deliver the swats.

The principles discussed in this book suggest that corporal punishment normally should not be used. The undesirability of coporal punishment is not because it necessarily is a cruel form of punishment administered out of hatred (although such often may be the case), but rather because so many other more effective ways are available to eliminate undesirable behaviors.

Disadvantages of Corporal Punishment as Compared to Other Possible Forms of Punishment

1. Corporal punishment emphatically teaches only what not to do. Corporal punishment cannot readily be teamed up with negative reinforcement to teach some desirable behavior at its termination. The punishment ceases when the pain stops hurting. Therefore, no way is easily available to see to it that the child is performing a desirable behavior when the punishment ceases. (When working with rats, to give them painful electrical shocks until they perform the desired behavior is possible, then terminate the shocks. But few people would seriously want to do anything analogous when administering corporal punishment to human beings.)

2. One finds extreme difficulty in making the severity of the punishment proportionate to the seriousness of the offense.

3. Corporal punishment is less likely than other forms of punishment to bear some relationship to the offense. The exception to this rule is physically punishing a child for physically hurting someone else. ("You hit your little brother. Now how do you like it when I hit you?") Such an approach might indeed prove effective, but even here there is some irony in trying to teach a child not to hit others by hitting that child.

4. Probably corporal punishment will lead to aggressive behavior on the part of the child and/or others watching the punishment. One can imagine a child thinking, "If Daddy solves his problems by hitting me, then that's the way I'll solve my problems too."

5. Corporal punishment is more likely to lead to suppression of spontaneous behaviors, to avoidance behaviors, and to retaliatory behaviors on the part of the child.

6. Among older children especially, peer prestige associated with spanking often supplies a positive reinforcing value which far overshadows the punishing effect of the spanking.

7. Corporal punishment is too often used by the parent/teacher while in a state of frustration, exasperation, or anger.

8. Perhaps the most important argument against corporal punishment is that is is hard to integrate it with negative reinforcement at its termination (see Chapter 3).

The main point is that many other more effective control techniques are available which do not embody the previous disadvantages. Hastily or angrily administered corporal punishment saves the teacher or parent--and perhaps most importantly the child--from having to diagnose the misbehavior and seek a course of remediation of the undesirable behavior.

The Appropriateness of Physical Punishment--When and with Whom

Physical punishment makes the most sense with children who are truly incapable of responding to any other form of punishment. The simple assertion that "These children have been beaten all their lives; all they understand is a good paddling," does not make a child fit this criterion. In fact, many children about whom this assertion is made respond to nothing other than punishment primarily because nobody has tried anything with them other than harsh punishment or unmitigated license. The fact that these children still need to be punished after a whole lifetime of having been dealt with through harsh punishment in itself suggests that a new approach might be in order. Such children might indeed respond to some of the other techniques discussed in this book.

Some children however do not respond to _any_ form of punishment other than physical punishment. Physical punishment is a primary form of punishment--it requires no conceptual learning to know that it hurts to be struck. In two cases for example, physical punishment seems to be a very appropriate punishment: in the cases of very young children and autistic children (who respond very little to language and engage in self-destructive behaviors). If teaching a baby not to play in the street or with electrical outlets is important, the only way this behavior can be accomplished effectively is by striking them when they do such things. A relatively light smack does no permanent damage to the child, but serves to make him or her sorry to have done whatever precipitated the smack. By pairing a loud shout of "No!" with the smack, the word "No!" will very rapidly become a conditioned aversive stimulus and often eliminate the need for striking the child. The work of Lovaas with autistic children is discussed briefly elsewhere in this book.

Corporal Punishment - Is It Inhumane?

A final point that needs to be made is that possibly all the rhetoric about corporal punishment misses the point. If what we are concerned about is being humane to children and punishing only in an effective manner, then corporal punishment is not necessarily the worst way to punish children. For example, public ridicule from a parent or teacher is often viewed by children as being much more cruel than a privately administered spanking. As a matter of fact, with most older children, it's the humiliation aspect of a spanking that hurts more than the actual physical impact. I've asked numerous students to name the worst teacher they've ever had, and ten times as many students mention a teacher who made fun of them as mention a teacher who spanked them. Likewise, depriving a child of privileges or learning opportunities for prolonged periods of time is going to hurt the child in a very real sense much more than even a rather severe bruising on his or her body.

Passing laws against spanking children does not eliminate the physical abuse of children. Spanking is only one possible form of corporal punishment. Lifting a child up by the hair, squeezing an arm severely, forcing a child to kneel for a long period of time holding heavy weights--these and other forms of punishment are sometimes harsher to the child's body than a carefully administered swat with a hand or paddle. The only effective way to insure humane treatment of children is to develop attitudes of love and concern for children.

SUMMARY

A detailed discussion of seven specific kinds of punishment has been presented in this Chapter. Each kind has been an example of one of the three basic types of punishment or a combination of these basic types. The general guidelines for punishment (discussed in Chapter 2) are applicable to each of these specific kinds of punishment. In addition, unique aspects of each of the kinds of punishment were discussed. The cautions and guidelines discussed will make the implementation of these strategies more effective when the need for them arises.

Chapter 6

AVOIDING THE PUNISHMENT TRAP

* *

CONTENTS:
The Punishment Trap
How to Overcome the Punishment Trap
Punishing Ourselves for Punishing
Reinforcing Constructive Alternatives to Punishment
Analyzing Your Management Strategies
Think Before You Punish!
Reinforce Your Improvements
Avoiding Accidental Punishment
Summary

* *

Objectives of Chapter 6

After reading this Chapter, you should be able to

(1) describe what is meant by the punishment trap.

(2) identify two major tactics for overcoming the punishment trap and describe how to implement these techniques.

(3) describe techniques for analyzing your management strategies.

(4) identify techniques for avoiding the accidental use of punishment.

One of the outstanding features of punishment is that it often has very desirable effects which occur <u>immediately</u> and <u>emphatically</u>. This immediate and emphatic success often may be evident to the punisher even when the long-range effects of the punishment actually may be the exact opposite of the intended outcome. Because of this high probability of immediate apparent success, people often are strongly reinforced for using punishment as a control technique.

THE PUNISHMENT TRAP

Specifically, we are often <u>negatively reinforced</u> (See Chapter 3) for using punishment. For example, a child might be bothering us (aversive situation); and the aversiveness goes away if we simply send the child to his or her room, if we strike the child, or if we make a sharp comment to the child. Thus, since we have been reinforced for punishing the child, we therefore are more likely to punish again in the future--even though some other technique, such as finding the child something constructive to do, might have been more effective in the long run. This excessive reliance on punishment as a control technique can be referred to as the "Punishment Trap." We become "trapped" by punishment in the sense that its immediate attractiveness beguiles us into ignoring more effective techniques.

An unreasonably hasty recourse to punishment therefore is quite unwise. Punishment has all the undesirable side effects discussed in Chapter 2. Chiefly, the simple fact that a child lives in a constant atmosphere of punishment--especially when that punishment is not combined with positive reinforcement--is likely to make that child more inhibited than we would wish.

HOW TO OVERCOME THE PUNISHMENT TRAP

So here's the problem: we want to avoid the unreasonable use of punishment. How can we best accomplish this goal? Since we want to teach ourselves what <u>not</u> to do (not to punish inappropriately), the principles discussed in this book would suggest that we could <u>punish ourselves</u> for the misuse of punishment. This is often a good idea, and we'll discuss ways to do this; or we could reinforce ourselves for management strategies which are incompatible with punishment. Since punishment (even of oneself) may be accompanied by undesirable side effects, the tactic of reinforcing positive management strategies often is preferable to that of punishing inappropriate strategies.

A major problem that we shall have to deal with is that the reinforcement we feel for using punishment often is immediate: the undesired behavior goes away immediately, and the undesirable side effects of our punishing behavior become apparent only later. The more positive strategies, on the other hand, while relatively free from such side effects, are likely to provide us with reinforcement only in the more remote future. One of the main problems dealt with in this Chapter therefore is how to make reinforcement for the appropriate use of punishment or for the use of positive management strategies more <u>immediately</u> available.

PUNISHING OURSELVES FOR PUNISHING

To use punishment to prevent punishment may sound farfetched, but it works. The idea is to make your use of punishment at least mildly aversive to yourself. If you view the <u>act</u> of punishment as aversive, you'll think twice before using it; and if some other technique is available which is not aversive, you'll be inclined to use that technique instead.

One way to make the act of punishment aversive to yourself is <u>to involve yourself in the punishment</u>. If a teacher requires a child to stay after school as a form of punishment, the teacher might assign himself or herself the boring task of sitting there watching the child instead of going down to the teachers' lounge for some sparkling conversation or out to the golf course for a quick game.

Another way to make punishment aversive to yourself is to require yourself to do some unpleasant task every time you use punishment. For example, you might require yourself to sit down and write out a detailed report to yourself every time you use punishment. (Some police officers who have to fill out detailed reports whenever they discharge their firearms swear they'll never fire a shot.)

Other similar possibilities exist. If you use such techniques, you'll find that your readiness to use punishment will decrease. Also you'll find that often you'll be able to tell a child quite sincerely, "This punishment hurts me as much as it hurts you." A major problem however is the possibility of overgeneralization through suppression of desirable uses of punishment. If you're not careful, you'll find punishment so aversive that you'll avoid it even in the many instances when it is an entirely appropriate technique. Such over-inhibition would be a disservice both to yourself and to the child for whom you are caring. Because of this tendency toward over-inhibition, punishing yourself for punishing should be used with discretion, and only in conjunction with the positive techniques discussed next.

REINFORCING CONSTRUCTIVE ALTERNATIVES TO PUNISHMENT

Anticipate problem situations, plan how you can avoid them or handle them by employing the techniques in Chapter 4, and then reinforce yourself for the successful implementation of your plan. If your plan doesn't work as well as it should have, change the plan, and reinforce yourself both for making a new plan and eventually for your attempt to implement it. Likewise, you should reinforce yourself for coming <u>closer</u> to using positive techniques than you have come in the <u>past</u>. The idea is to find out when you normally use punishment; then, when the situation is about to arise, activate your positive plan of action. The self-analysis tactics discussed next will help you accomplish this implementation.

ANALYZING YOUR MANAGEMENT STRATEGIES

The first step in implementing plans to avoid the punishment trap is to focus ahead of time on potential punishment situations and find a way to adjust your behavior appropriately when such situations arise. This planning often can be accomplished by spending a week or so simply recording when you punish. For example, one elementary school teacher filled out the chart in Table 6.1. The kind of chart in Table 6.1 should be filled out as soon as possible after punishments occur. If necessary, filling out the chart can be delayed until the end of the day; but longer delays result in forgetting information. The description of the punishment on the Table should be as specific as possible. By analyzing such observational data, a teacher might make some astonishing but useful discoveries. For example, 80% of the teacher's punishments might be directed towards a single set of three children <u>only when they play together</u>. Or punishments might occur more frequently during arithmetic period than during any other time of the day. Another possibility is that the teacher might punish almost entirely when seated at the desk in front of the room. Such information will tell the teacher where to begin in attempting to minimize inappropriate punishment and to make appropriate punishment more effective.

Likewise, a father might fill out such a chart for a week and discover that he punishes primarily when his son is in the living room alone with him, and more specifically when the father is watching television. The father might therefore wonder why he rarely punishes when others are present or when the television is off. This analysis would probably lead to strategies for reducing the father's punitive behaviors.

Table 6.1. A Sample Punishment Chart.

Day: Mon., Jan. 17

Child Punished	Time	What did Child do?	What was I doing?	Type of Punishment
Bart Anderson	Roll Call	Threw spit wad at Jane	Sitting at desk.	Time out.
Smitty	Arith	Snatched Jane's purse.	Working at board.	Time out.
Smitty	Arith	Snatched Jane's purse.	"	No recess.
Carla J.	Arith	Copying from Barb.	Sitting at desk.	Do 20 problems extra.

THINK BEFORE YOU PUNISH

One of the main benefits of such an analysis of the punishing situations which occur in your weekly routine is that simply by focusing on them, you'll often start to minimize punishing behaviors. Many punishments, you'll probably notice, occur automatically. You tend to punish almost by reflex, without even thinking about it. The main secret in minimizing your punishing behaviors is to force yourself to <u>think</u> before you punish.

Stop punishing automatically. Find some specific way to make yourself think before acting. If you know when the problems are likely to occur, you can give yourself reminders in such situations. A chart such as that in Table 6.1 will help identify such target situations. The principle of thinking before punishing can be seen at work in three examples.

Example of a Self-Analysis:

Mr. Jablonski felt that he was punishing his third graders too often. By analyzing his behaviors for a week, he discovered that he punished most during arithmetic class. He decided to write the word <u>THINK</u>! in large letters on his bookmark. Then he made it a rule for himself to write down on the bookmark the name of each child he punished during arithmetic class before punishing that child. His punishments dropped by 80% within a week, and the problems formerly requiring punishment dropped similarly.

Example of a Use of Signals to Minimize Punishment:

Miss Peters used her time-out room a lot, and it occurred to her that maybe she used it <u>too</u> much. She wanted to find a way to cut down on sending children to the time-out area, but she wanted to do this without anybody else knowing what she was doing. So every day she simply wrote some ridiculous word in large letters over the time-out room. Nobody else ever guessed why she did this--although many tried--but whenever she looked at the time-out room and saw a word like AARDVARK glaring at her, she could not help but realize that she was supposed to think of something! Her use of the time-out room dropped by over 50% with no increase in misbehaviors.

Examples of Using Punishment Itself as a Signal:

    Mr. Jones had three children. He found himself punishing them constantly. In order to break his punishment habit, he decided to use the very act of punishment as a signal for reinforcement. Every time he punished one of his children, he required himself to find three occasions for reinforcing the children. This initially resulted in an increase in positive reinforcement and eventually in a reduction of punishment.

    The big trick is to force yourself to <u>think</u> before you punish. If you think about it and then decide that punishment is the right approach, <u>then</u> punish. If you think of a better approach, use that approach instead. In addition, as the next section will suggest, reinforce yourself in some way both for thinking and for implementing the appropriate strategy after thinking about it.

REINFORCING YOUR IMPROVEMENTS

Find some way to reinforce yourself for either <u>thinking</u> or for <u>implementing an alternative strategy</u>. Don't demand 100% performance before you reward yourself: reinforce an improvement from 0% to 10% thinking, if that's where your improvement program starts.

Your reward can be anything. For some parents or teachers, merely receiving feedback that they are going in the right direction is quite reinforcing. Such concrete reinforcement often can be provided by charts and graphs. The chart in Table 6.2 was designed by a mother of two small children who was making a major effort to <u>think of alternatives</u> before punishing her children. At the end of each day, she thought back and counted the number of times she had <u>wanted</u> to punish them. She recorded this total for the morning and for the afternoon under "Potential Punishment Situations" on the chart. Then she determined whether or not in each of these punishment situations she had <u>thought</u> of an alternative to punishment. She entered the number of times she had remembered to think on the chart; and in order to make comparisons easier, she computed the "Percentage of Thinking" by dividing the number-of-situations into the number-of-times-thought. In addition, each day she transferred this data recording her progress to the graph in Figure 6.1. This graph shows that she made progress in the morning, but not in the afternoon during that week. Such information was extremely useful to her in deciding what strategies to continue and what to change for the next week.

Other reinforcers might be to

1. buy something for yourself if you reach a goal.

2. watch a favorite show on TV only if you reach your goal.

3. eat a favorite dinner only if you reach the goal.

4. skip correcting papers if you reach your goal.

A token system often works quite well for parents and teachers. Give yourself a "point" every time you meet your goal of eliminating haphazard or inappropriate punishment. Then when you get fifty points, give yourself a reward. Take a point for meeting daily goals, two points for doubling the goal, and maybe even lose a point if you fall far short of the goal. A good idea is to give yourself a point for recording the data promptly each day since this act of recording is extremely important.

Table 6.2. Sample Alternative Strategy Chart.

	Potential Punishment Situations		Thought of Alternative Strategy
Mon. a.m.	10	N	5
		%	50%
Mon. p.m.	20	N	5
		%	25%
Tues. a.m.		N	
		%	

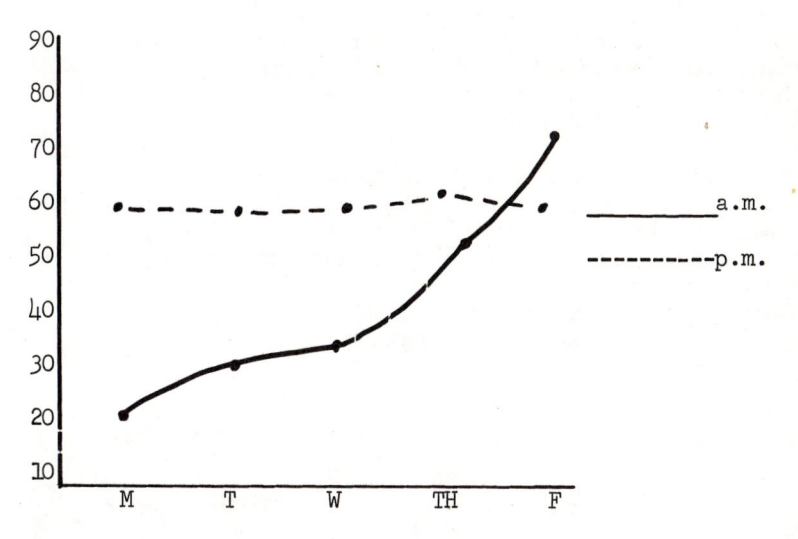

```
90
80
70
60  ·----·----·----·----·     ——————— a.m.
50                            ---------- p.m.
40
30
20
10
    M    T    W    TH    F
```

Figure 6.1. Sample Alternative Strategy Graph

Remember: your goal is _not_ necessarily to eliminate punishment. Punishment is often essential. Your goal is to eliminate _haphazard_ or _inappropriate_ punishment and to replace it with effective techniques.

AVOIDING ACCIDENTAL PUNISHMENT

Punishment reduces behavior: it teaches what _not_ to do. If we accidentally punish desirable behaviors, we often inadvertently help accomplish exactly the opposite outcomes that we would like to see happen. One of the main thrusts of this book is to help you avoid such mistakes. The following is a short list of questions which will help you systematically examine the possibilities wherein accidental punishments will occur, and to prevent their occurrence.

1. What unpleasant things happen to the person/group I'm concerned with? Do these things happen to them as a result of some desirable or at least neutral behavior? (Type I Punishment)

2. What pleasant things cease or are taken away from them? Are these things taken away because of some desirable behavior they perform? (Type II Punishment)

3. What things that I promise them (or promise I'll try to get them) don't materialize? Does this failure to obtain what they want happen because of something desirable that they do? (Type III Punishment)

If your answer is "Yes" to any of the above questions, the children are likely to perceive themselves as being punished for their desirable behaviors, and therefore will stop the desirable behaviors in the hope of getting what they want. This accidental punishment happens much more often than most people realize. By being aware of this possibility ahead of time, you can avoid many unfortunate mistakes.

SUMMARY

This chapter does <u>not</u> tell you not to punish, but rather not to abuse the technique of punishment. Punishment works. Punishment is a powerful technique. Individuals have strong inclinations to become lazy or careless and to use punishment too quickly. Punishment is not "evil." In many cases it's the <u>best</u> technique to use. But the important thing is to <u>THINK</u> before you punish. Make certain the punishment is the appropriate technique. If punishment is not appropriate, don't use it. If punishment <u>is</u> appropriate, use it effectively. (If you use it effectively, you'll wind up using it less often in the long run.) When you use punishment, <u>ALWAYS</u> combine it with reinforcement of some desirable behavior.

Chapter 7

SUMMARY -- WHEN SHOULD I PUNISH ?

****

CONTENTS: The Positive Role of Punishment
How We Punish Ourselves by Refusing to Punish Others
When Punishment Should NOT Be Used
Using Inappropriate Techniques by Accident
Comparison of the Various Techniques for Eliminating Behaviors
Deciding What To Do
Summary

****

Objectives of Chapter 7

After reading this Chapter, you should be able to

(1) describe how refusal to punish may actually reduce your use of positive reinforcement strategies.

(2) identify three situations in which punishment should NOT be used.

(3) identify examples of accidental misapplication of the techniques discussed in this book.

(4) identify the comparative advantages and disadvantages of the techniques discussed in this book to eliminate behaviors.

This book does not insist that you should spend a great deal of time eliminating undesirable behaviors. Quite the contrary, the purpose of this book is to enable you to eliminate the undesirable behaviors, when elimination is appropriate, as rapidly and efficiently as possible, so that you can return to what the business of child rearing and education is really about--developing desirable behaviors. I would feel very badly if readers of this book would decide to use these techniques to simplify their lives merely by keeping children in line and suppressing their behaviors while teaching them nothing. Such a shortcut to a simple life is not what the book recommends.

THE POSITIVE ROLE OF PUNISHMENT

The aversive techniques discussed in this book upset many people. Most of us would rather use positive techniques as opposed to aversive techniques. But the simple fact is that some children are able to ignore all positive reinforcers that we offer them, whereas aversive stimuli are much harder for these children to ignore. Autistic children, for example, can almost totally ignore any reward you offer them: pounding their heads on the wall is often all they seem to really want out of life. Earlier we have been shown that a few very mild but aversive electrical shocks impinge on the existence of such children and help make them capable of responding to positive reinforcement. Autistic children, it can be agreed, are rare enough to be considered an exception; but the same principle can be applied to many "normal" children. For example, when I was teaching high school English, I had a student in my class who absolutely refused to do anything, no matter what incentives or rewards I would offer him. I had reason to believe I was offering a pretty good course, but all he wanted to do was "put in his time" until the bell rang and then go out and do his thing with his friends. I went up to him one day and stated, "Look, everybody has to do something in this course. Either you do something during class, or we both sit here for an hour after school till you do something." He did nothing, and we sat after school. The third day he realized he could get out of this whole "Mickey Mouse" business simply by completing an assignment, which was actually an enjoyable assignment anyway; and so he finished it after only a half hour. The next day he completed an assignment during class and continued to do so thereafter. He eventually became one of my better students and apparently benefitted from the experience. Was it really inhumane to disturb his existence and coerce him into doing something? You'd have a hard time convincing me.

HOW WE PUNISH OURSELVES BY REFUSING TO PUNISH OTHERS

If punishment is definded as the contingent presentation of an aversive situation, it seems clear to me that many parents and teachers are punishing themselves by refusing to use punishment under any circumstances. Certain undesirable behaviors can be eliminated quite efficiently by punishment. These same undesirable behaviors can be eliminated only with great difficulty, if at all, through more positive techniques such as extinction and positive reinforcement of incompatible behaviors. When we try to attack these behavior problems through the more positive techniques, we are likely to fail. If failure does occur, we are presented with an aversive situation: the continuation of the often obnoxious, undesirable behaviors which need to be eliminated. In such cases, we actually are being punished for employing the more positive techniques; and as a result of this punishment we are actually less likely to use positive techniques in the future. Why should we be punished for using desirable techniques? We would be much better off to approach the child with the strategy of using positive techniques whenever possible, but when necessary making judicious use of punishment and negative reinforcement. By doing so we would stand a much better chance of being successful and a much lower chance of being punished personally. In the long run we would be better able to use much more positive reinforcement. This idea is summarized in Table 7.1.

The concept explained in the above paragraph might sound farfetched at first, but think back or look around and see if I'm not right. I have met a very large number of new teachers who have gone forth promising to be "Mister Nice Guy" and found this attempt at niceness a very frustrating experience. Within a year these same teachers become some of the most reactionary, repressive teachers I can imagine.

What I do recommend is that if you do punish--especially harshly--think about it. Are you really accomplishing what you want to accomplish? Is there a better way to teach what to do as well as what not to do? In general, give precedence to positive techniques when you gain something by doing so or lose nothing. When you do punish, do so in such a way as to minimize the negative side effects.

Table 7.1. Self-punishment Through Refusal To Punish.

	The following pattern of parent/teacher behavior often occurs:
Stimulus:	The parent/teacher has behavior problems with the child.
Response:	The parent/teacher tries to solve the problems using positive reinforcement techniques alone (no punishment).
Punishment:	The positive reinforcement program fails. The child continues to misbehave.
Stimulus:	The parent/teacher is frustrated by the continued misbehavior.
Response:	The parent/teacher resorts to harsh punishment.
Negative Reinforcement:	The behavior problems immediately and sharply decrease. (There may be long-range negative side effects--but remember, we're dealing with a frustrated parent/teacher who wants out of a bad situation.)
Result:	The parent/teacher resorts to positive reinforcement less and less in the future (because it has failed) and resorts to punishment more and more (because it has worked).
	The author recommends the following ideal parent/teacher behavior pattern instead:
Stimulus:	The parent/teacher has behavior problems with the child.
Response:	The parent/teacher tries to solve the problems using <u>both</u> punishment for the undesired behavior and positive reinforcement for an incompatible desired behavior.
Negative Reinforcement:	The program succeeds. The misbehavior ceases.
Result:	The parent/teacher continues to use the combined technique (because it has worked).

WHEN PUNISHMENT SHOULD NOT BE USED

Punishment used in certain situations actually would be a bad idea. In everyday life, punishment frequently is misused in such specific situations. As you read the following guidelines, undoubtedly you will be able to think of times where you have either used punishment in a similar situation or have witnessed someone else doing so. Re-analyze such situations to determine whether or not punishment really worked effectively in those situations. The following are specific occasions when punishment should not be used.

Specific Guidelines for When Not to Punish

1. Don't use punishment when the undesirable shortcomings (negative side effects) outweigh the advantages to be gained. In addition to obvious immediate side effects, the positive advantages of using punishment have to be weighed against the following two considerations:

    a. What is good for the individual must be at least harmless to the well-being of the group of which the individual is a member and vice versa.

    b. What is good for the individual at the present moment must be at least harmless with regard to long-range goals for that individual.

   If you think about it, you'll probably notice that these two rules are impossible to observe all the time. But they do serve as useful guidelines in evaluating negative side effects.

   This guideline is extremely important. Since punishment (especially severe punishment) works efficiently and rapidly, many parents and teachers have a tendency to use it too hastily. For example, ridiculing a child for showing up late for Sunday School is a form of punishment which is likely to stop tardiness, but also is likely to build up avoidance attitudes towards religion; and since a major purpose of Sunday School is to develop favorable attitudes toward religion, the teacher would be sacrificing long-range goals for short-range convenience.

   If the negative side effects do outweigh the positive advantages, either use an alternate punishment strategy, such as reinforcing incompatible behaviors, or look for a more suitable punishment strategy.

2. Don't use punishment when you are trying to teach a person what to do. Teaching a person what to do is simply not what

punishment is designed to accomplish. Punishing a child will not teach that child to read. Punishment will however teach him or her not to look out the window. And if the child stops looking out the window, a better chance may occur for other appropriate reinforcement techniques to be applied to teach reading skills. But even with regard to looking out the window, some cautions are in order:

"You can't see out the windows from back here - now maybe you'll learn to read."

a. Looking out the window may not be the cause of the reading problem. The child may be unable to read because of a motivation problem, emotional problems at home, or a visual perceptual problem.

b. Punishment may cause the child to dislike reading if reading is inappropriately reinforced.

3. Don't use punishment unless you use it in conjunction with another technique. There are exceptions to this rule. For example, sometimes your sole intention is to teach a child what not to do: Don't play on the railroad tracks. Don't put your fingers in the electrical outlet. Don't bite electrical wires. In most cases however when a person is punished for an undesirable behavior, that person should be

given an opportunity as soon as possible to perform an appropriate behavior and should be reinforced for this appropriate performance.

USING INAPPROPRIATE TECHNIQUES BY ACCIDENT

One of the most useful things you can learn from this book is the awareness that all the techniques in the book often are applied <u>by accident</u>. If you do nothing else but recognize such situations where techniques are being accidentally applied and stop reinforcing undesirable behaviors or punishing desirable behaviors, you will have profitted a great deal. Table 7.2 lists several examples of the accidental inappropriate administration of the techniques discussed in this book.

Table 7.2. Examples of Accidentally Accomplishing Inappropriate Results.

Type I Punishment: Accidentally administering an aversive stimulus.

A teacher publicly praises a child, but the child views this praise as an embarrassment in front of his or her peers.

A person is given more work to do after he or she does an extremely good job.

Type II Punishment: Accidentally removing a privilege.

A child cleans up his or her room very promptly, but then is sent to bed early because of having finished the task.

People have to stay overtime at a meeting if they ask any questions.

Type III Punishment: Giving a new privilege and then accidentally removing it.

A half hour before the class is scheduled to end the professor says, "If there are no further questions, this class will be dismissed." There are never any further questions.

A mother tells her son she'll take him to the zoo on Saturday, but then she doesn't do this because they have to take care of the next door neighbor's children instead.

Negative Reinforcement: Accidentally terminating an aversive situation at the wrong time.

Sending a child to the time-out area and then letting him or her out after the child has obnoxiously begged to be let out for ten minutes.

Keeping a child after school, but then letting that child go home after he or she has made up a fabulous lie about a sick mother.

Positive Reinforcement of Incompatible Behaviors: Accidentally reinforcing a behavior which is incompatible with the one you would really like to develop.

Reinforcing a child for playing chess to the extent that the child no longer studies for school.

A parent reinforces a child for playing around the house, with the result that the child never learns to get along with other children.

A mother buys candy for her son at the supermarket whenever he cries, and so the child never has to ask politely for candy.

Extinction: Accidentally withholding reinforcers which would maintain a behavior.

A teacher always calls on one child first, with the result that nobody but this one child ever volunteers.

Table 7.2 continued.

A teacher's only reinforcement for spelling success is giving a prize to the person who wins the spelling bee. As a result, only the five or six who have a chance to win learn to spell.

A wife cooks excellent meals, but no one ever compliments her.

<u>Satiation</u>: Accidentally administering a specific reinforcer until it loses its reinforcing value.

A wife makes her husband's favorite meal every night for two months.

A teacher uses candy to reinforce reading behavior and eventually the children stop working for the candy.

A teacher tells his students that they can read any book they wish as soon as they complete their grammar assignments. He does this every day. The students say they would rather do something else once in a while.

<u>Discrimination Training</u>: Accidentally teaching a child that it's OK to perform a certain behavior, provided the child does it only in certain situations. (Eliminating the behavior in only part of the target situations.)

Students work quietly when the teacher is present, but become very rowdy when a substitute teacher is present.

<u>Stimulus Change</u>: Accidentally removing a stimulus which had prevented a behavior or accidentally introducing a stimulus which will trigger a behavior.

The mother says, "Don't sneak into the refrigerator and eat any candy." When she returns, the candy is gone. (She has added a triggering stimulus.)

The students do their own work on tests when the teacher stands in front of the room and looks at them. But when she sits at her desk and reads, the students copy from each other. (She has removed a preventing stimulus.)

<u>Counterconditioning</u>: Accidentally associating a pleasant or neutral subject with an aversive stimulus.

A college student hates a psychology course because it takes place in a smoke-filled room.

Table 7.2 continued.

A student builds up a dislike for anything associated with "school subjects."

<u>Systematic Exclusion (Time-Out)</u>: A student is accidentally excluded from a situation that he or she considers aversive rather than pleasant.

A student who hates English class finds that he or she can be sent out of the room if that student causes a disruption.

A child who dislikes school finds that he or she can be suspended for smoking.

<u>Negative Practice</u>: Accidentally administering a reinforcer to the point where it actually becomes aversive to the person.

A child who once said he or she liked poetry is required to read poetry every day during English class.

A child who used to tinker with the piano is forced to practice two hours a day.

<u>Vicarious Punishment</u>: When one person is punished, an observer inappropriately applies the aversive situation to him or herself.

One child is punished for arguing disrespectfully with the teacher. Another child thinks the punishment was for asking questions and stops raising his hand in class.

COMPARISON OF THE VARIOUS TECHNIQUES FOR ELIMINATING BEHAVIORS

This book has discussed punishment and eight other techniques for eliminating behaviors. In addition, in this book seven specific kinds of punishment have been examined in greater depth. Table 7.3 attempts to synthesize this information.

Note that all the advantages and disadvantages are relative (1) to the technique to which they are being compared and (2) to the severity with which any technique is implemented. Thus, while extinction is considered in Table 7.3 to have the advantage of being relatively free from negative side effects, it must be noted that it has fewer side effects than punishment but more side effects than discrimination training. Likewise, ignoring a child for three weeks (extinction) will have more severe side effects than expressing even strong disapproval (punishment) on a single occasion.

Nevertheless, Table 7.3 provides a useful summary of advantages, disadvantages, and guidelines in the implementation of each of these techniques.

Table 7.3. Techniques for Reducing or Eliminating Behaviors.

Technique	Advantages	Disadvantages
Punishment	Rapid. Efficient. Long lasting. Teaches what <u>not</u> to do.	Only teaches what <u>not</u> to do. Causes avoidance behaviors. Reduces spontaneity. Models aggressiveness. Often merely suppresses the behavior. Encourages retaliation. Encourages self-derogation.
Time-Out	Can be combined with negative reinforcement. Relatively free from negative side effects. Long lasting.	The child is removed from the learning situation.
Response Cost	Works nicely with negative reinforcement of desirable behaviors.	May be viewed as unfair. Child may give up.
Negative Practice	Long lasting. Works for involuntary behaviors.	Often viewed as harsh.
Overcorrection	Long lasting. Works for involuntary behaviors.	Often viewed as harsh.
Corporal Punishment	Can be delivered immediately. Over with quickly.	Little chance for negative reinforcement. Models aggressiveness. Often harsh. Often administered by frustrated persons.
Positive Reinforcement of Incompatible Behaviors	Teaches what <u>to</u> do. Free from negative side effects.	Less efficient in eliminating behaviors. Does not teach what <u>not</u> to do.

Guidelines to Overcome Disadvantages

---
1. Combine with positive reinforcement of a desirable behavior.
2. Punish a behavior, not a person.
3. Specify the behavior that is being punished.
4. Use non-punitive modes of punishment (especially Type III).
5. Punish early in the behavioral sequence.
6. Match the severity to the seriousness of the misbehavior.

---

1. Keep the time-out period as brief as possible.

---

1. Allow the person to have accumulated a sufficient supply of reinforcers.
2. Penalize sparingly and fairly.
3. Allow opportunities to regain lost reinforcers.

---
1. Use primarily with volunteers.
2. Use primarily for automatic, uncontrollable behaviors.

---
1. Use rarely.
2. Use primarily for automatic, uncontrollable behaviors.

---
1. Use only when a more effective technique is not available.
2. Do not delay administration.

---

1. Be sure the behavior *is* in fact incompatible.
2. Use in conjunction with punishment.

Table 7.3 continued.

Extinction	Relatively free from negative side effects.	Sometimes not all reinforcers can be withheld. Initial increase in behavior. Intense misbehaviors. Occasional reward. It's hard to ignore behaviors. Self-reinforcing behaviors. New misbehaviors can emerge.
Satiation	Free from negative side effects.	Effects temporary. Sometimes takes a while for a behavior to reach satiation.
Discrimination Training	Free from negative side effects. Teaches what _to_ do.	Often a difficult learning task. Takes a long time if used alone.
Differential Reinforcement of Other Behavior (DRO)	Often very fast.	Often temporary.
Differential Reinforcement of Low Rates of Behavior (DRL)	Avoids over-suppression of behavior.	Takes longer than punishment.
Stimulus Change	Free from negative side effects.	Often only temporary.
Counterconditioning	Works with automatic (involuntary) behavior.	Mere conditioning: no cognitive content.

Table 7.3 continued.

Guidelines (Con't.)

---

1. If you need rapid, complete elimination, use punishment instead.
2. Count on a slight initial increase if you can afford it.
3. Combine with positive reinforcement of a desirable behavior.
4. Stick completely to the extinction schedule. If you have to give attention, give aversive--not pleasant--attention.
5. Practice ignoring misbehaviors.
6. If new misbehaviors emerge, run a new extinction schedule for them.

---

1. Use only for behaviors which are likely to satiate quickly.
2. Combine with positive reinforcement of alternate behaviors.

---

1. Combine with extinction or punishment.

---

1. Use only if you are desperate.

---

1. Use only when you want to minimize but not eliminate behavior.

---

1. Use only at specific signal for the misbehavior.
2. Combine with positive reinforcement for a desirable behavior.

---

1. Use only for irrational behaviors (such as fear).

DECIDING WHAT TO DO

Figure 7.1 is a gross over-simplification, but it serves a useful purpose. Figure 7.1 superficially gives the impression that you simply could feed a few pieces of data into a computer and the machine would within a few seconds tell you what to do about a behavior problem with which you are dealing. We all know that this solution is not the case. The purpose of Figure 7.1 is not to provide _a priori_ simplistic answers to behavior problems, but rather to provide a basis for generating and evaluating ideas for what to do next. Figure 7.1 merely diagrams many of the main ideas presented in this book. This diagram gives you some simple decision rules; and these decision rules can provide you with some tentative strategies which need to be supplemented and often overridden by common sense and by the data previously reviewed in Table 7.3 of this chapter.

FIGURE 7.1

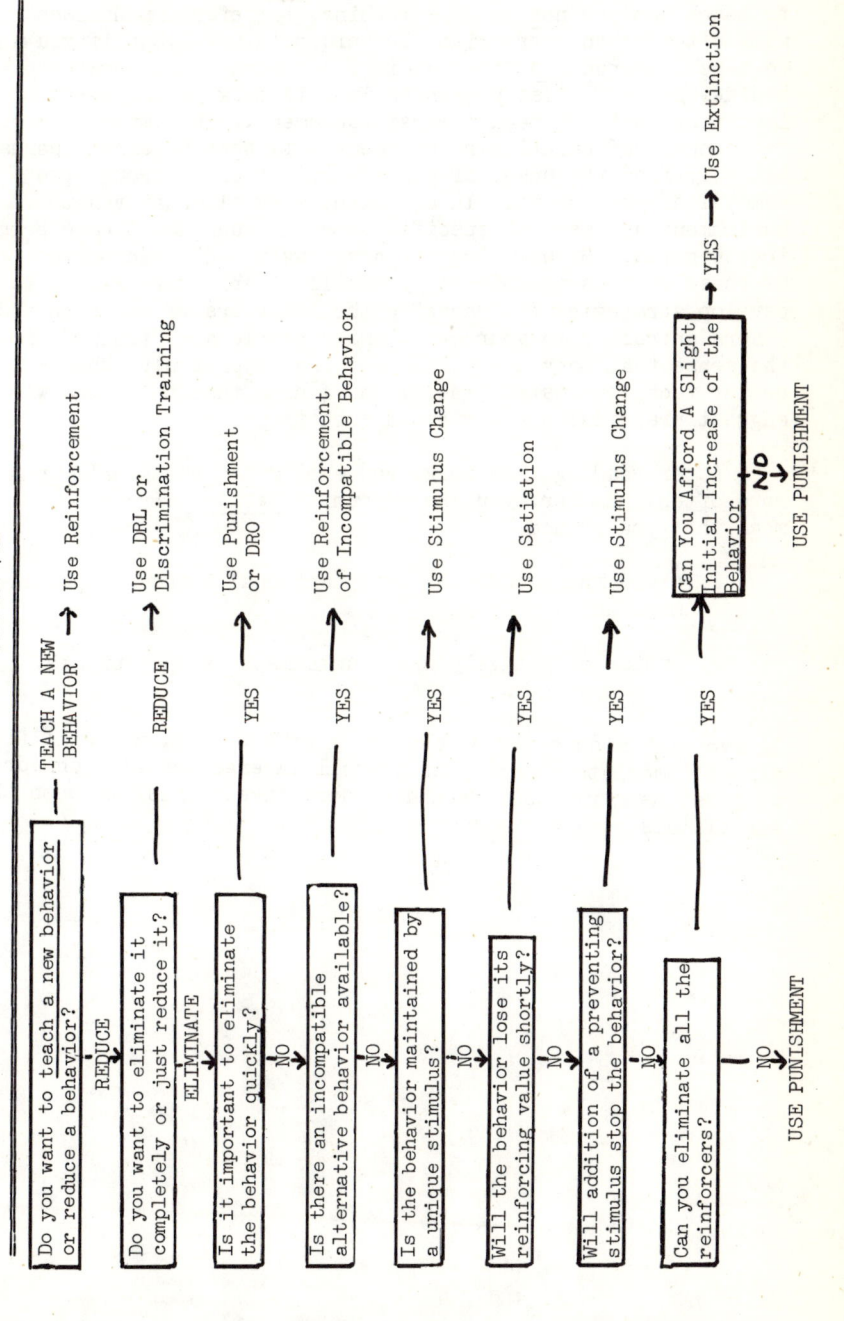

```
                                    ┌─ TEACH A NEW ──→ Use Reinforcement
                                    │   BEHAVIOR
┌──────────────────────────────┐    │
│ Do you want to teach a new   │────┤
│ behavior or reduce a         │    │
│ behavior?                    │    │  REDUCE
└──────────────────────────────┘    └──────→ Use DRL or
                                              Discrimination Training
┌──────────────────────────────┐
│ Do you want to eliminate it  │──── ELIMINATE
│ completely or just reduce it?│
└──────────────────────────────┘

┌──────────────────────────────┐         YES
│ Is it important to eliminate │──────────────→ Use Punishment
│ the behavior quickly?        │                 or DRO
└──────────────────────────────┘
            │ NO

┌──────────────────────────────┐         YES
│ Is there an incompatible     │──────────────→ Use Reinforcement
│ alternative behavior         │                 of Incompatible Behavior
│ available?                   │
└──────────────────────────────┘
            │ NO

┌──────────────────────────────┐         YES
│ Is the behavior maintained   │──────────────→ Use Stimulus Change
│ by a unique stimulus?        │
└──────────────────────────────┘
            │ NO

┌──────────────────────────────┐         YES
│ Will the behavior lose its   │──────────────→ Use Satiation
│ reinforcing value shortly?   │
└──────────────────────────────┘
            │ NO

┌──────────────────────────────┐         YES
│ Will addition of a           │──────────────→ Use Stimulus Change
│ preventing stimulus stop     │
│ the behavior?                │
└──────────────────────────────┘
            │ NO

┌──────────────────────────────┐         YES   ┌─────────────────────┐  YES
│ Can you eliminate all the    │─────────────→ │ Can You Afford A    │─────→ Use Extinction
│ reinforcers?                 │               │ Slight Initial      │
└──────────────────────────────┘               │ Increase of the     │
            │ NO                                │ Behavior            │
                                                └─────────────────────┘
        USE PUNISHMENT                                    │ NO
                                                      USE PUNISHMENT
```

SUMMARY

The point developed in this book is that punishment is a powerful technique for teaching what not to do. If you want to teach someone not to do something, therefore, punishment will often be an appropriate technique to use. But if you want to teach a person to do something, you have to do something besides punish. Also presented in this book is the very important topic of negative reinforcement. The importance of the concept of negative reinforcement is that a person learns not only from the onset of punishment but also through the removal of punishment. In addition, many alternatives to punishment and several specific types of punishment have been investigated. By weighing the advantages and disadvantages of these various techniques, you will be able more easily to develop strategies for managing the behaviors of children and others entrusted to your care. Many people are "trapped" in the sense that they use punishment inappropriately, when a better technique is available; and I hope that this book will suggest practical ways to avoid such traps.

After reading this book, you should not necessarily punish more often. Rather, you should punish better. By this I mean that you should

1. avoid the accidental or intentional misuse of punishment and

2. punish effectively when punishment is appropriate.

By avoiding misuse and by punishing effectively, you will find almost immediately that your overall interaction with children will become more positive and constructive. This has been the aim of this book.

****

APPENDIX A

REVIEW QUESTIONS

****

REVIEW QUESTIONS

The following questions are based on information discussed in this book. These questions are presented in random order, rather than chapter by chapter. Answers follow each question. In addition to the correct answers, a commentary is given on each of the inaccurate responses. The numbers in parentheses refer to the page number of the rationale for the correctness or inaccuracy of a response.

The best way to go through these review questions is to do them one at a time and then check the correct answer immediately. Several items deal with each topic; and by checking your accurate and inaccurate answers as you go, you can use these questions as a programmed review of the entire book.

If you get a question right, assume that you know the information and do not bother looking up the cited page number. However, if you get an item wrong, figure out why you got it wrong. If the error was merely ambiguity in the item, don't worry about it. But if you missed an answer because of an actual mistake, refer back in the text to both the page number cited for your incorrect answer and the page number cited for the correct answer. This review should help you understand the principle in question.

1. Which of the following is NOT an example of punishment?

   a. Ignoring a child having a temper tantrum.
   b. Expressing verbal disapproval of a child's misbehavior.
   c. Taking a teenager's driving privileges away for the weekend.
   d. All of the above are examples of punishment.

   Answer and Commentary

   a. Correct. This example is of extinction, not punishment.
   b. Wrong. This is Type I punishment, assuming that the child finds this disapproval to be aversive.
   c. Wrong. This is Type II punishment, assuming that the teenager wants to drive the car that weekend.
   d. Wrong. Example a is extinction, not punishment.

2. Punishment and negative reinforcement differ in the following manner: punishment causes a behavior to decrease, whereas negative reinforcement causes a behavior to increase. (Answer true or false.)

a. True
b. False. Both cause the behavior to <u>increase</u>.
c. False. Both cause the behavior to <u>decrease</u>.
d. False. Punishment causes a behavior to <u>increase</u>, whereas negative reinforcement causes a <u>behavior</u> to decrease.

Answer and Commentary

a. Correct.
b. Wrong.
c. Wrong.
d. Wrong. This statement is the exact reverse of the actual situation.

3. An activity which is perceived as punishment by Susie will always be perceived by Susie as punishment; but it is possible that it will be viewed as positive reinforcement by Barbara. (Answer true or false.)

a. True.
b. False. It will not necessarily be perceived by Susie as punishing on other occasions.
c. False. It is highly probable that what is perceived by Susie as punishment also will be perceived by Barbara as punishment.

Answer and Commentary

a. Wrong. For the reasons stated in <u>b</u>.
b. Correct. What is a punishment for a person is that which he or she perceives to be aversive. Such perceptions will vary from person to person and from time to time.
c. Wrong. For the reasons stated in <u>b</u>.

4. Do both extinction and negative reinforcement normally cause a behavior to decrease?

a. Yes, both.
b. No, only extinction causes behaviors to decrease.
c. No, only negative reinforcement causes behaviors to decrease.
d. No, neither causes behaviors to decrease.

Answer and Commentary

a. Wrong. <u>b</u> is correct.
b. Right.
c. Wrong. <u>b</u> is correct.
d. Wrong. <u>b</u> is correct.

Use the following information for Questions 5 and 6:

Billy is eight years old and wants to play baseball with his brothers and his friends who are all 12. The big kids won't let Billy play, and so Billy sits down on second base and cries. Since they cannot play their game while Billy is sitting there and they are afraid that if Billy keeps on crying their mothers will think they are picking on him, the big kids finally give in and let Billy play.

5. What technique are the big kids accidentally employing to encourage Billy to cry and sit on second base in the future?

   a. Positive reinforcement
   b. Negative reinforcement
   c. Punishment
   d. Modeling
   e. Shaping

   Answer and Commentary

   a. Correct. They are giving Billy something that he likes.
   b. Wrong. Negative reinforcement is the removal of something aversive. The big kids are not removing something aversive from Billy, but rather are giving him something that he likes (playing baseball).
   c. Wrong. Punishment refers to the contingent presentation of an aversive situation. The big kids are doing nothing aversive to Billy. Moreover, punishment would have the effect of reducing a behavior, and the big kids are encouraging the base-sitting behavior in Billy.
   d. Wrong. Modeling refers to rewarding or punishing someone else with the hope that the viewer will vicariously learn from the other person's reward or punishment.
   e. Wrong. Shaping refers to the deliberate attempt to develop a new behavior which the learner previously was incapable of performing.

For Question 6 use the information about Billy provided prior to Question 5.

6. What technique is Billy using to get the big kids to let him play with them in the future?

   a. Positive reinforcement
   b. Negative reinforcement

c. Punishment
   d. Extinction
   e. Desensitization

   Answer and Commentary

   a. Wrong. He is not giving them anything pleasant for letting him play, rather he is taking away something unpleasant (his presence on second base) if they let him play. If Billy would let the big kids play with his brand-new baseball for letting him play, then this would be positive reinforcement.
   b. Correct. He is bothering them and then removes this unpleasant bothersomeness as soon as they let him play.
   c. Wrong. Punishment only reduces behaviors; it does not teach what _to_ do. Billy _is_ punishing the big kids for trying to play without him in that area. Reducing that behavior does not guarantee that the big kids will adopt a friendlier behavior. Note that the big kids also could have gained negative reinforcement by playing baseball without Billy, if they would have gone somewhere where Billy was not allowed to go.
   d. Wrong. Extinction would be effective only if the big kids wanted some reinforcer (such as attention) from Billy, and Billy would withhold this reinforcer unless they would let him join the game.
   e. Wrong. Desensitization refers to a process for eliminating irrational fears.

7. Which of the following is designed to cause a behavior to _decrease_?

   a. Positive reinforcement.
   b. Negative reinforcement.
   c. Extrinsic reinforcement.
   d. Token reinforcement.
   e. None of the above.

   Answer and Commentary

   a. Wrong. Positive reinforcement causes a behavior to _increase_.
   b. Wrong. Negative reinforcement causes a behavior to _increase_. It is _not_ synonymous with punishment.
   c. Wrong. Extrinsic reinforcement is merely a type of positive reinforcement and therefore causes a behavior to _increase_.

d. Wrong. Token reinforcement is merely a form of positive reinforcement and therefore causes a behavior to _increase_.
e. Correct. The only sense in which any of these would eliminate a behavior would be through reinforcement of an incompatible behavior (p.   ), but even in this case the learner would be merely learning _to_ do something else, not specifically learning what _not_ to do. Reduction of a behavior is therefore merely a side effect of _a-d_.

8. Which of the following is a valid reason to _avoid_ using physical (corporal) punishment?

    a. It models aggressive behavior to the child being punished.
    b. It causes a rapid reduction in the undesired behavior.
    c. It is difficult to incorporate the technique of negative reinforcement into the punishment program.
    d. Both _a_ and _c_ are correct.
    e. All of the above are correct.

    Answer and Commentary

    a. This answer is correct, but so is _c_, below.
    b. This might happen, but there is no reason to refer to this as a disadvantage.
    c. This answer is correct, but so is _a_ above.
    d. Correct.
    e. Wrong. (See _b_ above.)

9. If a student has an irrational fear of speaking to girls, what would be the most useful technique to help him overcome his fear?

    a. Negative practice.
    b. Negative reinforcement.
    c. Systematic desensitization.
    d. Punishment.
    e. Overcorrection.

    Answer and Commentary

    a. Wrong. This is a form of punishment.
    b. Wrong. This technique increases behaviors by removing aversive circumstances.
    c. Correct. This is a technique designed to reduce irrational fears by having the person gradually go through a hierarchical series of steps which bring that person close to performing the feared activity.

d. Wrong. Punishment reduces voluntary behaviors; but this irrational fear is an automatic, involuntary behavior.
e. Wrong. This is a form of punishment.

10. A "satiation effect" occurs which can reduce the effectiveness of both (1) extrinsic and (2) intrinsic reinforcers.

    a. True.
    b. False. Satiation occurs only with extrinsic reinforcers.
    c. False. Satiation occurs only with intrinsic reinforcers.
    d. False. Satiation occurs only with punishment.

    Answer and Commentary

    a. Correct.
    b. Wrong. There is no reason to assume that satiation is limited to extrinsic reinforcers.
    c. Wrong. Satiation is even more likely to occur with regard to extrinsic reinforcers.
    d. Wrong. Although a phenomenon similar to satiation occurs when a person gets used to some form of punishment, there is no reason to say that this is limited to punishment.

11. Once a behavior has undergone extinction, it will never again occur in that person.

    a. True
    b. False

    Answer and Commentary

    a. Wrong. If a person has not learned an alternate behavior, the chances are relatively high that if the reinforcers become available again, the extinguished behavior will return.
    b. Correct.

Use the following information for Questions 12 and 13:

Barbara has trouble completing her science experiments because she spends a great deal of time looking out the window to see George jogging around the athletic field during his gym class. Mr. Einstein, the teacher, tells Barbara that she can no longer sit near the window, but will have to sit instead on the other side of the room. From the new location Barbara will be unable to view the athletic field. She will be allowed to return to her original place as soon as she turns in a correct paper on the experiment she is supposed to be doing. Mr. Einstein plans to repeat this process any time he finds Barbara slacking off on her assignments by looking out the window.

12. Requiring Barbara to sit on the other side of the room is a form of punishment.

   a. True.
   b. False. It's a form of extinction.
   c. False. It's a form of negative reinforcement.
   d. False. It's a form of social reinforcement.

   Answer and Commentary

   a. Correct. This is Type II punishment.
   b. Wrong. Extinction refers to the withholding of the reinforcer which has been maintaining a behavior. Mr. Einstein goes beyond this by putting Barbara in a specifically unpleasant (aversive) situation.
   c. Wrong. Negative reinforcement refers to the removal of an aversive stimulus, whereas in this case Mr. Einstein is presenting an aversive situation.
   d. Wrong. Social reinforcement refers to a type of positive reinforcement. By taking away a privilege, Mr. Einstein is bothering Barbara, not doing something pleasant to her.

For Question 13 use the information about Barbara provided prior to Question 12.

13. Allowing Barbara to return to her seat as soon as she completes a correct assignment is an example of both (1) positive reinforcement and (2) negative reinforcement.

   a. True, both.
   b. No, only positive reinforcement.
   c. No, only negative reinforcement.
   d. No, neither.

   Answer and Commentary

   a. Correct. Barbara is positively reinforced by being allowed to watch George again, and she is negatively reinforced because she gets out of the misery of sitting on the other side of the room.

b. Wrong. See reasons in a.
   c. Wrong. See reasons in a.
   d. Wrong. See reasons in a.

14. In an ideal situation, when is the best time to terminate a punishment?

   a. When the behavior is completely extinguished.
   b. When the undesirable behavior ceases.
   c. When the person performs a desirable, alternate behavior.
   d. When the punishment reaches its full intensity.

   Answer and Commentary

   a. Wrong. In many cases this would result in continual punishment.
   b. Wrong. This response is better than a, but there is a better answer in an ideal situation.
   c. Right. This incorporates negative reinforcement for the desirable behavior with punishment for the undesirable behavior.
   d. Wrong. Punishment should be introduced at full intensity in the first place.

15. The "Punishment Trap" occurs because

   a. Children like to trick teachers into giving punishments which they actually enjoy.
   b. Teachers and parents often find punishment positively reinforcing.
   c. Teachers and parents often find punishment negatively reinforcing.
   d. Punishment actually encourages children to engage in retaliatory behavior.

   Answer and Commentary

   a. Wrong. Children probably do become adept at this technique, but it is unrelated to the "Punishment Trap."
   b. Wrong. While a few teachers probably do enjoy punishment (especially because of peer status), this is not the primary cause of the "Punishment Trap."
   c. Correct. The aversiveness of the children's misbehavior is removed at least for the immediate future when the teacher or parent punishes. Thus the punishment technique is reinforced by having something unpleasant taken away.

d. Wrong. While this is indeed one of the undesirable side effects of punishment (p.   ), it is not related to the "Punishment Trap."

16. Caroline pretends that she is sick and stays home from school on any days when she might have to give an oral report to her class. She apparently does this because she is afraid to speak in front of the class. Which of the following techniques would most likely help stop her feigned illnesses?

    a. Systematic desensitization.
    b. Punishment.
    c. Negative reinforcement.
    d. Satiation.
    e. None of the above would be likely to help.

    Answer and Commentary

    a. Correct. This is an irrational fear and is appropriately treated by desensitization.
    b. Wrong. Punishment would be likely to have the undesirable side effect of increasing her anxiety.
    c. Wrong. Nothing aversive could be removed contingent upon her desirable behavior.
    d. Wrong. There is no probability that her behavior will lose its reinforcing value.
    e. Wrong. (For reasons, see a.)

17. John comes home from the office and mentions to his wife that his secretary flirted with him but he successfully and heroically repelled her advances. His wife becomes upset and refuses to speak to John for the rest of the evening. Moreover, the next day she phones the secretary and tells her to keep her dirty hands off John. John finds this whole situation terribly embarrassing. What behavior of John's is most likely to be negatively reinforced?

    a. Flirting with his secretary.
    b. Telling his wife about his secretary's flirtations.
    c. Keeping quiet about future flirtations of the secretary.
    d. All of the above.
    e. None of the above.

    Answer and Commentary

    a. Wrong. This is the behavior that the wife is trying to punish, but she's actually missing the point and

punishing John instead for <u>telling</u> her about the flirtations.
   b. Wrong. This behavior is being punished. It is the thing that John will almost certainly <u>not</u> do in the future.
   c. Correct. Actually, John also could be negatively reinforced by preventing the secretary from flirting with him, but he can get out of the aversive situation (be negatively reinforced) most easily by just keeping quiet about what happens.
   d. Wrong. (For reasons, see above.)
   e. Wrong. (For reasons, see above.)

18. Mrs. Lopez wants her daughter, Juanita, to do neat papers in school. Therefore, whenever Juanita brings home her papers, Mrs. Lopez examines them for neatness. If the papers are sloppy, Juanita has to rewrite them before she can go out to play. Juanita's teacher has noticed that whereas most students in the class write essays of about 400 words, Juanita writes only about 25-word essays. What behavior of Juanita's in Mrs. Lopez punishing?

    a. Writing sloppy papers.
    b. Writing neat papers.
    c. Writing lengthy papers.
    d. Writing short papers.

    Answer and Commentary

       a. Wrong. This is what Mrs. Lopez <u>thinks</u> she is punishing, but she's not.
       b. Wrong. Juanita is actually likely to be negatively reinforced for writing neat (although short) papers.
       c. Correct. The worst thing that can happen to Juanita is that she will bring home a lengthy paper which her mother perceives to be sloppy.
       d. Wrong. This is actually the behavior most likely to be encouraged (through negative reinforcement).

19. Which of the following is NOT an example of punishment?

    a. A child who likes school is suspended from school for cussing.
    b. A child who appreciates his father's kind words is told by his father that his dad is ashamed of his behavior.
    c. A child who burps loudly to get his teacher's attention is told by the teacher that he will have to stay in the

time-out area (which he dislikes) for ten minutes every time the teacher hears him burp.
d. All of the above <u>are</u> examples of punishment.
e. None of the above are examples of punishment.

Answer and Commentary

a. Wrong. This is an example of Type II punishment.

b. Wrong. This is an example of Type I punishment.

c. Wrong. This is an example of Type II punishment.

d. Correct. (See above for reasons.)
e. Wrong. (See above for reasons.)

20. Mr. Rickoff is tutoring Samuel Smith in a one-to-one situation. Samuel is somewhat distractable, and so Mr. Rickoff has told him that every time he pays attention, Mr. Rickoff will give him a drink of pop from the can of pop he places on the table. At the start of the session, Mr. Rickoff says "Pay attention!" and Samuel immediately sits up straight and looks at him. Samuel gets his drink of pop. Two minutes later Samuel starts fidgeting, and Mr. Rickoff says "Pay attention!" Samuel straightens up and gets his pop. During each subsequent session, Mr. Rickoff uses the same technique; but Samuel still spends about 75 percent of the time fidgeting needlessly. What technique should Mr. Rickoff use to get Samuel to sit still quickly and with the fewest negative side effects?

a. Punishment.
b. Negative reinforcement.
c. Extinction.
d. Systematic desensitization.
e. Stimulus chance.

Answer and Commentary

a. Wrong. Punishment would be likely to have negative side effects.
b. Wrong. Negative reinforcement would have to involve punishment first, and therefore would involve the same side effects as punishment.
c. Wrong. Extinction would be likely to work very <u>slowly</u> if used alone.
d. Wrong. This is not an irrational fear.
e. Correct. Samuel has learned that the signal for the delivery of the reward involves a complex behavior. First Samuel has to cause Mr. Rickoff to say "Pay attention!" Then he has to straighten up. If he

doesn't fidget, Mr. Rickoff will never offer him a reinforcer. Mr. Rickoff should find a way to give Samuel the pop contingently but unpredictably.

21. Under which of the following circumstances would extinction be preferable to punishment?

    a. You have plenty of time to get rid of the undesirable behavior.
    b. You are in a hurry to get rid of the undesirable behavior.
    c. You want to minimize the probability that the child will avoid you (the teacher or parent).
    d. Both a and c are correct.
    e. Both b and c are correct.

    Answer and Commentary

    a. This is one of the advantages of extinction, but so is c, below.
    b. Wrong. If you are in a hurry, you should use punishment instead, since it is more efficient.
    c. This is one of the advantages of extinction, but so is a above.
    d. Correct. (For reasons, see a and c.)
    e. Wrong. (For reason, see b.)

Use the following information for Questions 22, 23, and 24:

Stanley comes home from school and tells his father that he got spanked by the teacher that day for breaking a school rule. Stanley's father says that Stanley should keep the school rules; and because he broke a school rule, he will have to spend the entire evening in his room with no record player or television.

22. For what behavior is Stanley most directly being punished by being confined to his room?

    a. For breaking the school rule.
    b. For breaking a societal rule.
    c. For telling his father what happened in school.
    d. For being a worse child than his father had hoped to raise.
    e. None of the above.

Answer and Commentary

a. Wrong. He would perceive himself as being punished <u>directly</u> for this by the <u>teacher</u>, but only <u>indirectly</u> by his father.
b. Wrong. This may have been what his father was trying to accomplish, but there is no reason to expect this to occur.
c. Correct. This is exactly what <u>caused</u> him to have to stay in his room.
d. Wrong. He may get a vague feeling of this, but there's no reason to expect it to be of paramount importance.
e. Wrong. (See above.)

For question 23 use the information about Stanley provided prior to Question 22.

23. For what behavior is Stanley being positively reinforced in the above example?

a. Keeping the school rules.
b. Telling his father the truth.
c. Breaking school rules.
d. Lying to his father about what happened in school.
e. None of the above.

Answer and Commentary

a. Wrong. From the above description, Stanley will at best be <u>negatively</u> reinforced for this.
b. Wrong. He is actually being <u>punished</u> for telling the truth.
c. Wrong. His father is trying to <u>punish</u> him for this, but it's quite likely that this "punishment" will have no effect on Stanley's behavior.
d. Wrong. Stanley is likely to be <u>negatively</u> reinforced for not telling his father the truth.
e. Correct. (For reasons, see above.)

For Question 24 use the information about Stanley provided prior to Question 22.

24. What behavior of Stanley's is likely to be <u>negatively</u> reinforced in the future?

a. Keeping school rules.
b. Lying to his father.
c. Breaking school rules.
d. Telling his father the truth.

Answer and Commentary

    a. Wrong. Stanley <u>could</u> do this, but there's an easier way to avoid punishment. He might do both <u>a</u> and <u>b</u>: try to keep the rules; and whenever he fails, lie to his father.
    b. Correct. This would be the most direct way for Stanley to avoid his father's wrath.
    c. Wrong. Breaking school rules will do nothing to eliminate the punishment from his father.
    d. Wrong. This actually will get him more punishment.

25. When would <u>extinction</u> be <u>least</u> likely to succeed in eliminating a behavior?

    a. When the child previously has been <u>punished</u> for the behavior.
    b. When the child previously has been <u>continuously reinforced</u> for the behavior.
    c. When the child previously has been <u>intermittently reinforced</u> for the behavior.
    d. When the child previously has been <u>negatively reinforced</u> for the behavior.

Answer and Commentary

    a. Wrong. This would be the <u>second</u>-best answer for the question. The reason it could have some validity is that the child <u>might</u> perceive himself as being negatively reinforced by the removal of the punishment. Answer <u>c</u> is more clearly correct.
    b. Wrong. After continuous reinforcement is when extinction works <u>most</u> efficiently.
    c. Correct. Intermittent schedules of reinforcement result in longer extinction periods.
    d. Wrong. It is the <u>schedule</u> of reinforcement, not the type of reinforcement, which determines the length of time needed for subsequent extinction.

26. A boring teacher who <u>discontinues</u> her lecturing when the class becomes rowdy is quite likely to <u>increase</u> the rowdy behavior in her class.

    a. True
    b. False

Answer and Commentary

  a. Correct. The students are being negatively reinforced for rowdy behavior.
  b. Wrong. (See above.)

27. Mr. Skinner is a chaperon at the school dance. He discovers that four students (Bob, Carol, Ted, and Alice) have been engaging in sexual intercourse in the teacher's lounge. Which of the following would be LEAST likely to help Mr. Skinner reduce such behaviors in the future?

   a. Positive reinforcement of incompatible behaviors.
   b. Punishment.
   c. Extinction.
   d. All of the above would work.
   e. None of the above would work.

   Answer and Commentary

   a. Wrong. Seeing to it that the students were having a good time doing other things would make it unlikely that they would feel a need to leave the dance to engage in promiscuous activities. Note, however, that if there is extremely easy access to the teacher's lounge, the alternate activities would have to be extremely reinforcing to override their current interests.
   b. Wrong. Some form of punishment probably would be the most effective single technique. Of course, punishment should best be combined with positive reinforcement of a desirable behavior; otherwise they will look for ways to circumvent the punishment.
   c. Right. It seems highly improbable that Mr. Skinner could withhold the reinforcers maintaining their behavior, since these reinforcers are inherent in the activity itself (cf. The Kinsey Report).
   d. Wrong. (See above.)
   e. Wrong. (See above.)

28. Davey is two years old and is playing with the electrical outlet. What should his mother do?

   a. Give Davey something better to do and reinforce that behavior.
   b. Punish Davey.
   c. Ignore the behavior.
   d. Reason with Davey about the dangers of electrical outlets.

Answer and Commentary

a. Wrong. This would not teach him to stay away from electrical outlets. If this is all his mother did, it is quite likely that Davey would play with sockets when he goes to someone else's house.
b. Right. Her intention is to teach him what not to do. She probably is not concerned about side effects. She might do both a and d, however, while punishing him.
c. Wrong. This could result in the child's death.
d. Wrong. The child probably is too young for his mother to rely on reason alone. She wants to teach him not to do something. She could reason while punishing him.

29. You are a sixth-grade student, and you like to see your teacher yell at the class. She yells whenever you leave your desk. If you want to strengthen her yelling behavior, what should you do?

a. Sit down every second or third time she yells at you.
b. Simply ignore her no matter how often she yells.
c. If she asks you quietly to be seated, do so.
d. Be seated as soon as she gives you a stern look.

Answer and Commentary

a. Right. This would be putting her on an intermittent schedule.
b. Wrong. You would be extinguishing her yelling behavior.
c. Wrong. You would be reinforcing a behavior incompatible with yelling.
d. Wrong. (Reasons same as c.)

30. Jason is three years old. The only word he says is "Whadda," which his parents interpret to mean "What's that?" Whenever Jason says "Whadda," his parents talk to him with great enthusiasm about whatever he is looking at. When his parents go to a counselor and ask what to do about Jason, he tells them to ignore his "Whadda" and to pay attention to any real words Jason says. Within three weeks, Jason develops a 90-word vocabulary and can talk in sentences. Why did Jason originally have only a one-word vocabulary?

a. He was positively reinforced for saying only one word.
b. He was negatively reinforced for saying only one word.
c. He underwent extinction when he said more than one word.

Answer and Commentary

a. Correct. He received social reinforcement for saying his one word.
b. Wrong. People who give this answer usually misunderstand what is meant by negative reinforcement. They think it refers to the strengthening of a bad behavior. This is not the case.
c. Wrong. His parents would have reinforced him for more words. He was just getting so much attention for his one word that he didn't feel a need to say more.

****

ANNOTATED

BIBLIOGRAPHY

****

ANNOTATED BIBLIOGRAPHY

(A Few Books for Further Reading)

This bibliography is not meant to be comprehensive. Rather, it lists just a few books that the reader might want to consult to do further reading in the area of punishment and behavior modification.

Books on the General Topic of Behavior Modification:

Bandura, A. Principles of Behavior Modification (New York: Holt, Rinehart and Winston, 1969). This book is widely regarded as the most authoritative source on the topic of behavior modification. It goes into the theoretical aspects quite deeply and presents a good deal of experimental data. This book probably is written more for the academic-oriented person (student or teacher) than for the "layperson," although it is not excessively complex.

Becker, W. C., Engelmann, S. and Thomas, D. R. Teaching 1: Classroom Management (Chicago: Science Research Associates, 1975). This book explores all areas of behavior modification. It is written in an easy-to-use semi-programmed format. It is oriented primarily toward classroom instruction.

Clarizio, H. Toward Positive Classroom Discipline (New York: Wiley, 1976).
This book explores all areas of behavior modification, but not in as much depth as the book by Becker, Engelmann and Thomas. It is easy to understand and is written primarily for teachers.

Craighead, W. E., Kazdin, A. E., and Mahoney, M. J. Behavior Modification: Principles, Issues, and Applications (Boston: Houghton Mifflin, 1976). This book gives a thorough and scholarly presentation on all aspects of behavior modification. In addition, it summarizes research on specific topics (anxiety, smoking, prisons, etc.).

Rimm, D. C. and Masters, J. C. Behavior Therapy: Techniques and Empirical Findings (New York: Academic Press, 1974). This book goes into behavioral techniques besides those usually labeled "behavior modification." It's extremely useful to the counselor and others who work on a one-to-one basis, but will also provide ideas for anyone else interested in correcting inappropriate behaviors.

Williams, R. L. and Long, J. D. _Toward a Self-Managed Life Style_ (Boston: Houghton Mifflin, 1975). This book is written at a very simple and clear level. It applies the principles of behavior modification to self-management. It discusses such problems as athletic skills, study behavior, and dieting.

Information Specifically Related to Punishment:

Campbell, B. A., and Church, R. M. _Punishment and Aversive Behavior_ (New York: Appleton-Century-Crofts, 1969). This book deals with punishment in considerable detail. However its usefulness is severely limited because it deals with very "basic" (mostly animal-related) research. It is definitely not for the "lay" reader.

Johnston, J. M. "Punishment of human behavior." _American Psychologist_, 1972, _27_, 1033-1054. This article contains the most extensive review available and analysis of research related to punishment. It analyzes methodological problems, research conclusions, and implications for future research. It's well organized and quite readable.

Other than Johnston's article, there is no really good single source on research applications to punishment. If you're interested in further research, your best bet is to look up the references in the works cited above by Johnston (1972); Bandura (1969); and Craighead, Kazdin, and Mahoney (1976). A journal which often cites research related to practical applications of punishment theory is the _Journal of Applied Behavior Analysis_.

****
INDEX

****

INDEX

A

Accidental negative
  reinforcement, 55-59,
  97, 155-156, 159, 160
  examples of, 129, 155-156,
    159, 160
Accidental positive
  reinforcement, 39, 132-136,
  159, 162
  examples of, 159, 162
Accidental punishment, 16-23,
  23, 128, 155-156, 158
  examples of, 11, 14-15,
    18-21, 21-23, 39-40,
    100, 129, 132-136
Aggression
  modeling of, 3-4, 25
American revolution, 21
Animals, 44
Arithmetic class, 29-30, 50,
  70-71, 118
Art class, 50
Autistic children, 84-85, 127
Aversive situations, 11, 13,
  59-60, 148
Aversiveness
  perception of, 148
Avoidance behaviors, 23-24,
  44-45

B

Babies, 53, 80-81, 161
Baseball, 149-150
Behavior
  retaliatory, 25
  sexual, 17, 55, 102, 161
  suppression of, 24
Behavioral constriction, 24
Behaviors
  avoidance, 23-24, 44-45
  escape, 45
  religious, 90-91, 130

Boredom, 65-67, 73-74
Bribes, 28-29

C

Careless work, 65-66, 97
Charts, 116, 117, 120-121
Cheating, 81-82, 90-91
Childbirth, 54-55
Children
  autistic 84-85, 127
  mentally retarded, 55
Class
  arithmetic, 29-30, 50,
    70-71, 118
  art, 50
  math, 28-29, 65-66, 68-69
  participation, 17, 18-21
  science, 152-153
Class participation, 17, 18-21
Cleaning up, 17, 64-65, 68-69
Corner
  sitting in, 39-40
Corporal punishment, 105-110,
  137, 151
Counterconditioning, 91-92,
  102, 133-136, 136
Covert punishment, 101-103
Creativity, 25, 36-37

D

Desensitization
  systematic, 91-92, 151, 155
Detention, 39-40, 114
Differential reinforcement,
  88-90
  DRL, 89-90, 137-142
    142-144
  DRO, 88, 137-142, 142-144
Discrimination training,
  86-87, 132-136, 142-144
Disruptive students, 17,
  80-81, 87, 89-90, 95, 99

171

Drinking, 56-57
DRL, 89-90, 137-142, 142-144
DRO, 88, 137-142, 142-144

E

Eating, 43, 102
English class, 17, 59-60,
   70-71, 127
Escape behaviors, 45
Extinction, 31-33, 75-85,
   132-136, 137-142, 142-144
Extrinsic reinforcement,
   27-30, 47

F

Feedback
  negative, 36-37
Friends
  playing with, 15, 16, 33-34,
   51-53, 59-60, 64-65,
   65-66, 72-73, 95, 149-150
Further reading, 63, 167-168

G

Graphs, 120-121
Grocery stores, 56-58

H

Haircuts, 31-32
Harsh punishment, 3-8
Headaches, 44
Homework, 72-73

I

Impersonal punishment, 33-35
Intrinsic reinforcement,
   27-31, 47

L

Laughing, 35-37

M

Manners
  table, 23, 64-65
Math class, 28-29, 65-66,
   68-69
Mentally retarded children, 55
Modeling, 30-33, 103-106
Modeling of aggression, 3-4,
   25
Mosquito bites, 44

N

Nail biting, 99
Negative feedback 36-37
Negative practice, 98-100,
   132-136, 137-142
Negative reinforcement, 43-60,
   102, 103, 113, 127, 132-136,
   153, 154
Nose-picking, 88

O

Overcorrection, 100-101,
   137-142
Overgeneralization of
   punishment, 24, 88, 115

P

Perception of aversiveness,
   148
Playing with friends, 15,
   16-17, 33-34, 51-53, 59-60,
   64-65, 65-66, 72-73, 95,
   149-150

Police, 18, 115
Positive reinforcement, 26-34, 43-44, 51-52, 63-74, 142-144
Positive reinforcement of incompatible behaviors, 63-74, 132-136, 137-142, 142-144
Practice
   negative, 98-100, 132-136, 137-142
Primary reinforcers, 29-30
Punish
   why people, 3-6, 129
Punishment
   accidental, 16-23, 23, 128, 155-156
   advantages of, 137-142, 158
   corporal, 105-110, 137-142, 151
   covert, 101-103
   disadvantages of, 137-144, 158
   harsh, 3-8
   impersonal, 33-35
   overgneralization of, 24, 88, 115
   severity of, 37-38
   side effects of, 23-26, 47, 68-69, 88, 113, 130
   Type I, 11, 13, 17, 18, 21, 22, 43, 49, 122-123, 132-136, 157
   Type II, 12, 13, 17, 43, 50, 78-79, 95-98, 122-123, 132-136, 153, 157
   Type III, 12, 13, 19-20, 38-29, 43, 68-69, 122-123, 132-136
   vicarious, 103-106, 132-136
Punishment trap, 113-123, 154

R

Racquetball, 102
Reading, 131
   further, 63, 167-168
Reasons why people punish, 3-6, 129
Recess, 12, 72-73

Reinforcement
   accidental negative, 55-59, 97, 133-136
   accidental positive, 39, 133-136
   differential, 88-90
   examples of, 129, 155-156, 159, 160
   extrinsic, 27, 47
   intrinsic, 27-30, 47
   negative, 39-56, 95, 96, 105, 117, 124, 139, 140
   positive, 26-34, 43-44, 51-52, 63-74, 142-144
   schedules of, 31-33, 76, 79-81, 160, 162
   token, 30-31, 72-73, 97, 120
   vicarious, 30-33
Reinforcers
   primary, 29-30
   secondary, 29-30
   social, 29-31
Religious behaviors, 90-91, 130
Response-cost, 97-98, 137-142
Retaliatory behavior, 25
Revolution
   American, 21
Ridicule, 33-35
Rudeness, 72-73

S

Satiation, 85-87, 132-136, 137-144, 142-144, 152
Schedules of reinforcement 31-33, 76, 79-81, 160, 162
School
   suspension from 97
Science class, 152-153
Secondary reinforcers, 29-30
Selecting a strategy 142-144
Self-analysis tactics, 116-123
Self concept 25
Severity of punishment, 37-38
Sexual behavior, 17, 55, 102 161

Shaping, 30-31, 120
Side effects of punishment 23-26, 47, 68-69, 88, 113, 130
Signals, 118-119
Sitting in corner, 39-40
Smoking, 91, 98
Social reinforcers, 29-31
Spanking, 3-4, 5, 25, 39, 44, 105-110, 158
Stores
  grocery, 56-58
Strategy
  selecting a, 142-144
Stealing, 101
Stimulus change, 89-91, 118-119, 132-136, 137-142, 142-144, 157
Students
  disruptive, 17, 80-81, 87, 89-90, 95, 99
Suppression of behavior, 24
Suspension from school, 97
Systematic desensitization, 91-92, 151, 155

T

Table manners, 23, 64-65
Tactics
  self-analysis, 116-123
Tattling, 12, 80-81
Teasing, 12
Tests, 46-47
Time-out, 57-58, 59-60, 95-97, 118, 132-136, 137-142
Token reinforcement, 30-31, 72-73, 97, 120
Training
  discrimination, 86-87, 132-136, 137-142, 142-144
Tree-climbing, 72-73
Type I punishment, 11, 13, 17, 18, 21, 22, 43, 49, 122-123, 132-137, 157

Type II punishment, 12, 13, 17, 43, 50, 78-79, 95-98, 122-123, 132-136, 153, 157
Type III punishment, 12, 15, 19-20, 28-29, 43, 68-69, 122-123, 132-137

V

Vicarious punishment, 103-106, 132-137
Vicarious reinforcement, 30-33

W

Walking, 47-50
Whining, 16-17, 56-58, 80-81
Work
  careless, 65-66, 97

ABOUT THE AUTHOR

Edward L. Vockell received a doctor of philosophy degree in educational research and psychology from Purdue University in 1972. He is presently an associate professor in the Education Department, Purdue University Calumet Campus, Hammond, Indiana.

Vockell's teaching programs involve developing applied educational psychology into the graduate program of teacher education of Purdue. Much of the material in this book has been field tested in his Advanced Educational Psychology course at Purdue and in his course on Behavior Modification.

Vockell has published widely in professional journals, including Developmental Psychology, American Educational Research Journal, and Exceptional Children. Articles by Vockell have covered such topics as research methodology, birth order, sex education of the mentally retarded, and behavior modification.

Another publication, Developing Racquetball Skills, applies the principles of educational psychology to learning the principles of the sport of racquetball.

Kirtley Library
Columbia College
Columbia, Missouri 65216